Harold Pinter

WILLIAM BAKER

continuum

Continuum International Publishing Group

The Tower Building   80 Maiden Lane
11 York Road   Suite 704
London SE1 7NX   New York, NY 10038

British Library Cataloguing-in-Publication Data
A catalogue record for this book is available from the British Library.

ISBN: 978-0-8264-9970-7 (hardback)
      978-0-8264-9971-4 (paperback)

Library of Congress Cataloguing-in-Publication Data

Baker, William, 1944–
Harold Pinter/William Baker.
   p. cm.
   Includes bibliographical references.
   ISBN 978-0-8264-9970-7 – ISBN 978-0-8264-9971-4
   1. Pinter, Harold, 1930- 2. Dramatists, English–20th century–Biography 3. Poets, English–20th century–Biography. 4. Authors, English–20th century–Biography. 5. Screenwriters–Great Britain–Biography. I. Title.

PR6066. I53Z5955 2008
822'.914—dc22
[B]   2008005642

Typeset by Newgen Imaging Systems Pvt Ltd, Chennai, India
Printed and bound in Great Britain by MPG Books Ltd, Bodmin, Cornwall

Contents

Acknowledgements   vi
Introduction   1

1. Growing Up   2
2. Ireland, Precarious Existence and Marriage   24
3. Early Plays   39
4. Success   52
5. Turning Points   67
6. The 1970s and 1980s   82
7. The 1990s and Beyond: Political Engagement   104
8. Conclusion: Cancer, the Nobel Prize, Mutations of   130
   Mortality, Poetry

Notes   139
Bibliography   140
Index   155

Acknowledgements

In a book of this nature, many debts have been incurred. I'd like to thank Professor Donald Hawes for his judicious observations on the text and Anna Sandeman of Continuum for being such an understanding publisher and encouraging me initially to write the book for the Writers' Lives Series. Thanks are also due to Jayne Crosby-Lindner for her patience and good humour whilst helping in the preparation of the text. In the field of Harold Pinter studies I have especially benefited from the work of Michael Billington (I have particularly drawn upon citations from Pinter found in the new and updated edition of his excellent *Harold Pinter* published in 2007), the late Martin Esslin, Steve Gale, Francis Gillen, Alastair Macaulay and Susan Hollis Merritt. Thanks are also due to Judy Daish Associates, Craig Raine, editor of the splendid journal *Areté*, and of course to the great Harold Pinter, to whom this work is a tribute. Last but by no means least, my heartfelt thanks to my wife Rivka Baker for once again tolerating my obsession with the life and work of Harold Pinter.

Discussions and sessions at the "Viva Pinter" conference held at L'Université Jean Moulin 3 in March 2007 proved especially helpful and I would like to thank the organizer Professors Brigitte Gauthier and Alain Barrat for inviting me. Discussions, sessions and meetings at the Europa Theatre Prize Symposium held in Turin in March 2006, and an invitation to speak on Pinter's poetry at the University of Wales in Bangor in March 2007, proved to be most helpful. I would like to thank Professor Helen Wilcox, her husband and Ian Davidson and other colleagues at Bangor for making the visit so useful. Thanks are also due to respective Departmental Chairs and Deans at the University Libraries and the Department of English at Northern Illinois University for granting me leaves of absence for travel purposes and a sabbatical leave during 2006–2007 to work on Harold Pinter and other projects.

Introduction

This book is a comprehensive reassessment of all of Pinter's work and amplifies the present author's 1973 monograph *Harold Pinter* (Baker and Tabachnick, 1973). This drew upon Pinter's early background to reveal the ethnic origins of Pinter's output through *The Homecoming* (1965). The work argued that Pinter remained the supreme poet of the Hackney proletariat. The present book examines Pinter's output from his earliest work to the early twenty-first century, the receiving of the Nobel Prize for Literature, a seemingly successful fight against throat cancer, and apparent renunciation of dramatic writing to refocus on his poetry. The study draws upon neglected and obscure publications, prose work and letters. These are fully documented in my and John C. Ross's *Harold Pinter: A Bibliographical History* (2005). It consequently provides a comprehensive account of Pinter's total work in the areas of plays and sketches for the stage, radio and television, screenplays, poetry, fiction, non-fiction prose, essays, articles and public speeches, published letters to newspapers, magazines, his interviews printed in newspapers and magazines, the miscellaneous minor pieces, collaborative writings and editing, and other materials.

Pinter obviously has been the subject of much attention, but that critical focus has generally been on one particular aspect of his work, for instance, on his drama, or to a more limited extent, his film scripts, or his biography. None have comprehensively, thoroughly examined his total oeuvre and placed it in the perspective of his upbringing and personal experiences. None have in detail taken into account his archival record now at the British Library or the fact that he continually writes from experience. The present book takes into account all these aspects of Pinter's genius.

Chapter One
Growing Up

Harold Pinter was born at 19 Thistlewaite Road, Hackney, London, on 10 October 1930, the only child of Hyman (Jack) Pinter and Frances née Moskowitz. Jack Pinter was a ladies' tailor who eventually, in spite of the inherent insecurities due to cyclical ups and downs in the trade, developed his own tailoring business in the neighbouring Stoke Newington.

Although an only child, Pinter was from a large family with on both his father and mother's sides lots of cousins, aunts and uncles. His grandfather, Jack's father, Nathan born in Poland in 1870 (d. 1939) arrived in London in 1900 alone, fleeing from anti-Jewish persecution. He returned to bring his wife and family back to London, beginning in Stepney, close to the docks. Subsequently, the family moved further north to Amhurst Road in Stoke Newington. A retiring person, Nathan was employed in the clothing business focusing on women's wear. Nathan, according to family stories, was dominated by his domineering wife Fanny (née Baron/Bernstein). An attractive, diminutive lady born in Poland she was trained as a woman's hairdresser and in Stepney ran her own firm. Cleaning the house was not her forte; she preferred to listen to gramophone recordings by the great Austrian pianist Artur Schnabel (1882–1951), of Schubert and Beethoven. Harold, her grandson, had a soft spot for her. He claimed to have forgotten that Baron was her maiden name however Baron became the one he used when acting and in the initial draft of his only novel, the autobiographical *Dwarfs*, written between 1952 and 1956 but not published in prose form until 1990, he used Baron as the name for the central character Mark.

Nathan and Fanny had five children. Rachel the oldest was born in Poland in 1897 and died without children. The others were born in England. Sophie, the second, born 3 years later, excelled at the piano. She married Isidor Lipstein, a taxi driver. Taxi or cab drivers appear frequently in Pinter's work, most notably in *The Homecoming* (1964–1965), and review sketches such as, for instance, *Victoria Station* (1982). Driving London cabs in the period of 'The Knowledge' was a calling requiring a prodigious memory of London streets and landmarks. Many of the drivers were East Enders of Jewish origins. Isidor was a communist, skilled musician and fine chess player. Harold's father, born in 1902, was the first son, and there were two younger sisters, Mary and Dolly.

Pinter was interviewed by the Italian film director Roberto Ando in the late 1990s for an Italian television film on Pinter's life and work. Looking back at the turn of the twenty-first century at his family life, Pinter recalled that his father's family was very musical, especially his aunt Sophie who taught music; tragically she and her daughter, Pinter's cousin Sue, killed themselves in the early 1960s. His mother's side of the family, on the other hand, were very London, very tough and sturdy. His uncle on his mother's side ran a pub in Tottenham and was a real Cockney. His mother's father Harry Moskowitz, born in Odessa in the Ukraine with its large Jewish population and endemic anti-semitism, came to London around the turn of the century, after a stopover in Paris on his way. Like so many of the characters in Pinter's own plays who are illiterate, he survived off his intelligence, or wits. According to family tradition, his appearance was somewhat akin to Stalin's. This is born out by photographs taken at the 9 June 1926 wedding of Pinter's parents Jack and Frances. The photograph reveals that the Pinters were stocky and well built, a physical characteristic retained by Harold Pinter even in old age. His film appearances, for instance, as Sir Thomas Bertram in the 1999 Miramax Films' *Mansfield Park,* reveal the tall, over 6 feet, brooding, menacing quality of someone not to be messed about with rather in the model of Goldberg in *The Birthday Party* written in 1957.

Harry Moskowitz was self-employed, in the clothing trade. Using the name of Richard Mann, he at one time employed at least six or seven commercial travellers to sell his touched up clothing products. He met his first wife in South Africa. Following her death, he married Rose Franklin who was born in Poland. Pinter's mother Frances born in 1904 was the eldest of their four children. As a young girl she taught her father how to write and she kept his business accounts or ledgers for him. Ben was the second child. His wife Fay died from cancer. Following her death, he committed suicide and also took the life of their young daughter. The young Pinter loved the little child very much and their deaths deeply affected him.

Judah, the second son was born in 1907, was physically very strong, became a boxer using the name Joe Mann and is regarded as something of a black sheep within the Pinter family. There was another son, Lou, who was born in 1918. Apparently Judah was last seen following a blitz during the Second World War. Pinter recalls that he was around 11 at the time and his uncle Judah 'was just hanging off the back of this dustbin-van'. His 'Mother and grandmother looked up and I was agape'. In a scene straight from one of his own plays, funny, sad, surrealistic, but seemingly true, the family 'cried out loudly, "JUDAH!", and he looked at the three of us and unequivocally raised two fingers and the van went on . . . and we never saw him again . . . . I've been looking for him all my life and I've never found him.' (Cited Billington, 2007: 4).[1] Often in Pinter's work, characters will search for something; the most obvious case is in *The Caretaker*, written in 1959, where the tramp Davies claims that he has lost his papers, his identity and has to travel on various road routes around London in his search for them.

Pinter's mother's family was an extended, gregarious one, contrasted with his father's side. They were 'real Cockney barrel organ as compared to the piano-playing and Schnabel records of Granny Pinter and Aunt Sophie'. Pinter remembers especially large family Passovers, his grandmother Fanny playing a dominating role. He was also fascinated by the ancient Passover tradition of leaving a cup of wine for Elijah the Prophet who was supposed to drink it, but never did. Pinter in his interview with Roberto Ando claims to have never had any religious belief whatsoever at anytime and that his family disapproved of his position, but he wouldn't budge. The last time he went into a synagogue, apart from for weddings and funerals, was for his Bar Mitzvah which took place with the bombs falling all around, at the age of 13, in 1943.

Pinter's father Jack's family was Orthodox and throughout his life Jack retained his respect for Judaism. Jack died in 1997 and his death is the subject of one of Pinter's finest, most powerful poems, 'Death'.

This was 'written just after the registration of his father's death at Hove Town Hall'. Pinter and his father had a complex relationship, almost a violent one, disagreeing most notably over religion and politics. Jack like his son retained nostalgia for the East End. After going to live in the seaside Hove on the Sussex coast he would regularly go fishing in the Hackney and Stoke Newington rivers and canals rather than fish off the Sussex coast. There is a good deal of Pinter's father in Max in *The Homecoming* and in Davies in *The Caretaker*.

In spite of his numerous relatives, Pinter was a lonely only child. At the age of six he went to an elementary school near Clapton Pond (water especially in urban contexts in the shape of canals and ponds forms an idyllic quietude in his work). He had few friends, was introverted, morose and morbid and retreated into his little garden at home that he created at the age of eight and nine. There was a lilac tree and Pinter's first act of creation was behind the tree where he created imaginary friends and characters. His was a highly charged imagination and fantasy life: 'There was also – still is apparently – a laundry at the back of the garden so I was having this fantasy life with the laundry roaring away.' Later on in his teens with his school friends Pinter slept out in the garden which became the first of various idyllic worlds found in his work. In *The Dwarfs* 'The sun was setting. Lilac hung on the arched tree. The garden flickered' (cited *B*: 4–5).

The Late 1930s

However, even the London, the surroundings of Pinter's very early years, till War broke out in September 1939, was not idyllic. There was a latent shadow in the shape of Fascist marches on the predominantly Jewish East End. The marches and taunts of the anti-Jewish violent supporters of Sir Oswald Mosley (1896–1980), a charismatic leader and Nazi sympathiser, and the reactions to them, occurred a few miles from where the young Pinter lived. The Fascist insults and intent to march through the primarily Jewish area met with strong resistance. Such events left an indelible impression on those who participated in them and became essential ingredients of East End

Jewish folk memory. The events occurring just around the corner from Pinter's garden are recorded by creative artists and near contemporaries of Pinter such as Arnold Wesker (b. 1932) and Bernard Kops (b. 1926).

Wesker's *Chicken Soup with Barley* (1960) depicts the happenings of 4 October 1936. This was the day Mosley's supporters intended to 'march up to Aldgate, down Commercial Road to Salmon Lane in Limehouse' (17). They planned to hold a meeting in the Jewish heartland – Victoria Park. These events as seen through the vision of the 4-year-old Wesker have left an indelible imprint upon the mind of the very young sensitive child.

The slightly older Bernard Kops, who like Pinter and Wesker emerged on the national dramatic scene in the late 1950s and early 1960s, also records these events. In Kops' case, they are remembered in autobiographical prose form rather than dramatically. In *The World is a Wedding* (1963), Kops reflects upon on the autumn of 1936, when he was aged 10.

> Sometimes I ventured into the street, and I saw the policeman on their horses, protecting the blackshirts [Fascists], and swinging wildly at the people I knew. I saw my own brother, an onlooker, hit over the head with a truncheon, and he fell to the ground. But one of my big cousins saw it also. A few weeks later he and three brothers waited in a doorway in Jubilee Street, and when the policeman passed they did him up good and proper. They had remembered his number and shadowed him (37).

A universe of retribution, submerged violence and real violence also reverberates throughout Pinter's drama. In *The Birthday Party*, Stanley is fleeing from his past, pursuit and retribution. Inevitable violence lies in wait just around the corner.

So, in spite of idyllic memories, the world in which Pinter was born was far from idyllic. Hackney was just on the border country of the traditional East End. This constituted Aldgate, Bow, Shoreditch, Whitechapel, Bethnal Green and Stepney. By the time Pinter was born in October 1930, the Jewish population of these areas of North London, had grown from around 5,000 in 1880 to around 40,000 – a dramatic increase within a 50-year period. V. D. Lipman in his

Social History of the Jews in England 1850–1950 (1954) notes that 'North London Jewry (mainly in the Boroughs of Hackney, Islington and Stoke Newington) was notable for solid middle class respectability and religious conformity' (169). There were always internal fissions, conflicts as in Pinter's own family: between the artistic and the tough materialists; the religious and traditionalists and the secular; the dreamers, idealists and realists. In his moving poem 'Whatever Happened to Isaac Babel?' Bernard Kops' poem on the Jewish Cossack writer who disappeared in the 1930s, the poet asks, 'Whatever happened to Isaac Babel?| And if it comes to that- | whatever happened to those old men of Hackney| who sat around a wireless, weeping tears of pride| at weather forecasts from Radio Moscow?' (Bernard Kops' *East End*: 234). Indeed, a deep strain of political dissent also runs through Pinter's life and work. This emerged overtly since the 1970s after being latent and somewhat suppressed in his earlier work.

The programme note to the March 1959 Royal Court production of *The Room* and *The Dumb Waiter*, both written in 1957, reiterated Pinter's first extensive statement of his dramatic ideology. It initially appeared in *The Play's The Thing* (October 1958): 10–11, the previous year: 'There are no hard distinctions between what is true and what is false. A thing is not necessarily either true or false; it can be both true and false.' Of *The Birthday Party* Pinter said that the uncertainty, the menace, the fear have their origins not in 'extraordinary sinister people, but from you and me, it is all a matter of circumstances' (cited John Russell Taylor, 1962: 297).

The 'circumstances' political, ethnic, social, geographic into which Pinter was born, and grew up, provide a key to a comprehension of the uncertainty running throughout his work. The last years of the nineteenth century until the early 1920s experienced a population upheaval in the East End of London. Areas along the Whitechapel Road closest to the London docks, those renovated in the Docklands projects of the last two decades of the twentieth century, areas witnessing the full fury of the German aerial blitz on London in the early 1940s, were the conduit for the earlier waves of Eastern European Jewish immigration into London. The immigrants brought with them their own religious, social and ethnic traditions, leading to a new hybrid culture reflected in the growth of new idioms, inflections and speech rhythms reflected so often in Pinter's plays.

In the words of John W. Carrier in 'A Jewish Proletariat', in *Explorations an Annual on Jewish Themes* (1968): 'The East End was . . . the "stem" of a funnel through which a human population moved at various speeds and at various times.' The primary 'funnel areas' were 'Stepney, Shoreditch, Hackney and Stamford Hill.' The latter even at the end of the twentieth century remained a centre for a world within a world inhabited by deeply religious traditionalists dressed in the black hats and lengthy coats inherited from their Eastern European areas of settlements before coming to London. These areas were all stopping-off points on the Northwest passage to Golders Green and beyond. A contemporary wrote that he 'could remember when as a young man in the East End a move to Dalston or Hackney, was "like a move to green fields. You really thought you was on the up and up then."' For Carrier 'a move to Hackney was seen as a move up the social scale' (127–128, 138). It was even possible to escape into an idyllic back garden with a lilac tree and to create imaginary friends in an escape from a hostile, threatening world.

All was not idyllic. Apart from the followers of Mosley, there was the rise of Hitler in Germany, the storm clouds of a new war brewing, family tension and tragedies. In 25 February 1967 interview published in the *New Yorker*, Pinter recalled of his first 9 years, until the outbreak of the war: 'I lived in a brick house on Thistlewaite Road, near Clapton Pond, which had a few ducks on it.' More than 50 years later, on revisiting the area and the pond seeing the ducks, he quipped that they weren't the same ducks, but in any case vividly remembered the ducks. In this interview, Pinter observes, 'It was a working class area – some big, some run-down Victorian houses and a soap factory with a terrible smell, and a lot of railway yards. And shops. It had a lot of shops.' This characteristic Pinteresque repetitive pattern is followed by 'But down the road a bit from the house there was a river, the Lea River.' This river 'is a tributary of the Thames, and if you go up the river two miles, you find yourself in a marsh. And near a filthy canal as well. There is a terrible factory of some kind, with an enormous dirty chimney, that shoves things down to the canal.'

The idealised world, the world beyond the lilac tree was bordered by filth and the uncertain. Economic insecurity threatened to erode its very foundations. Pinter recalls that 'his father worked terribly hard. He worked a twelve-hour day, making clothes, but eventually lost the business and went to work for someone else' (the *New Yorker,* 25 February 1967: 34). Pinter's work is obsessed with this mixture of the idyllic and the non-idyllic, beauty and squalor, security and insecurity. Their roots are found in his childhood.

The War Years

A month or so before Pinter's ninth birthday, Britain declared war on Germany. Subsequently, Pinter and 24 other pupils from his elementary school were evacuated to a castle in Cornwall, away from the danger areas of London. Evacuation meant upheaval, a transition from the security of parents and the known to a world of strangers and an utterly different world. A war had come and life itself, its very fabric, the very surroundings, was transformed. Pinter had rarely seen the sea before or landscapes replete with flowers. He missed his parents tremendously, yet was aware somehow that something different and traumatic was occurring beyond his horizon and control. In short, the young Pinter was powerless.

During the first 6 months of the war nothing really happened, it was a phoney war. Subsequently, he saw planes in the air on their way to bomb London and aerial fights overhead. A real war was going on in London and elsewhere. The idea of actual death was very difficult to comprehend. One of his friends, Maurice, learnt that both his parents and his little sister had been killed in an air raid. Still life went on. Pinter remembers the teacher Mr. Nelson who came with the boys to the Cornish castle. He was a bully known as 'big fat Nelly with the cast-iron belly'. He had a 'a great habit of hitting you in the back with the knuckle of his middle finger extended' (cited *B*: 6).

In 1967 looking back on his time in Cornwall as a very young boy, Pinter pointed to the underlying insecurities disturbing him beneath the seemingly calm Cornish tranquillity.

I went to a castle in Cornwall – owned by a Mrs. Williams – with twenty-four other boys. It had marvellous grounds. And it was on the sea. It looked out on the English Channel, and it had kitchen gardens. All that. But it wasn't quite so idyllic as it sounds, because I was quite a morose little boy. My parents came down occasionally from London. It was over four hundred miles there and back, and I don't know how they made it. It was terribly expensive and they had no money. I came home after a year or so, and then I went away again – this time with my mother – to a place closer to London. (the *New Yorker*, 25 February 1967: 36)

On his return home again seeming security and total destruction surrounded him.

On the day I got back to London, in 1944, I saw the first flying bomb. I was in the street and I saw it come over . . . . There were times when I would open our back door and find our garden in flames. Our house never burned, but we had to evacuate several times. Every time we evacuated, I took my cricket bat with me (the *New Yorker,* 25 February 1967: 36).

Cricket became for the young Pinter, and remains with him, a symbol of peace and continuity following a period of flux and turmoil and the destruction of his own people. Speaking to Roberto Ando in 1998, Pinter said that all his family and friends knew that Adolph Hitler might invade. They had no illusions, they were well aware of what was happening to the Jewish population in Europe. They would have no chance at all of survival. 'That would be that.'

School Days

In September 1942 when he was just 12 Pinter started at the highly selective local Grocer's Company High School, Hackney Downs. He left in July 1948. At Hackney Downs he formed friendships lasting him for the rest of his life. Even at Pinter's Barmitzvah, his coming of age in the Jewish tradition, an occasion for enormous celebration and family gathering in spite of wartime and the Blitz, the German blanket bombing of London in October 1943, Pinter did something different. With the cash he received in envelopes from his aunts and uncle, he travelled from Hackney to the unknown world of central London, to the Charing Cross Road, and purchased a copy of James

Joyce's (1882–1941) revolutionary novel *Ulysses*. He then dipped into the novel that remains one of his favourite works.

Recalling his childhood in a November 2003 PEN discussion, Pinter says that his childhood is identified with a lack of money. He walked everywhere around Hackney and north London. Pinter remembers, for instance, walking a long way to the home of his school friend, and still a very close friend, Henry Woolf, to find only his parents in. They told Pinter to wait, offered him a cup of tea. While waiting, Pinter began to write a poem. Woolf's parents silently, almost reverentially, watched the young Pinter write. They respected the activity and Pinter's very act of writing gave them real pleasure. He would pop into friends' houses unannounced. They did not have telephones (certainly not cell phones) and no money for the bus, so he walked.

At Hackney Downs, Pinter was no recluse, formed friendships for life and was a very active sportsman. According to references in the *Hackney Downs School Magazine* in Christmas 1946, he came third in the 220 yards for under 16-year-olds. In the summer of 1947 again in School Sports he was third in the same event for his class. Towards the end of his school career, he was mentioned in football notes (Spring 1948) and then was awarded school cricket and football colours (Summer 1948). In the same issue he was mentioned in cricket notes, was the school vice-captain and achieved the best individual performance. Moreover, he equalled the school record in the 100 yards and set up a new school record in 220 yards and represented Hackney Downs in the 100 yards.

Cricket

Cricket remains for Pinter a favourite past time and reoccurs in his work as an idyllic metaphor, part of the memory of placid tranquil times. In an essay of Pinter's that first appeared in the *Daily Telegraph Magazine* on 16 May 1969 entitled 'Memories of Cricket' the factual and precise is conveyed in short staccato sentences. The heroes of youth are starkly contrasted: 'Hardstaff golden. Simpson dark'. Pinter describes 'Hardstaff and Simpson at Lords. Notts versus Middlesex, 1946 or 1947.' These two – hitting the ball across the smooth green playing field with agility, strength and grace, echo classical heroes. At the conclusion of the essay, Pinter makes the link between cricket and idyllic days gone forever. He recalls the 1946/1947 fight for the Ashes:

> I heard about Hutton's 37 on the radio. 7 a.m. Listened every morning of the 1946/7 series. Alan McGilvray talking. Always England six wickets down and Yardley 35 not out. But it was in an Irish kitchen in County Galway that, alone, I heard Edrich and Compton in 1953 clinch the Ashes for England. (*Daily Telegraph Magazine*, 16 May 1969, 25–26)

In three run-on lines entitled simply 'Poem' (1986), Pinter enshrines Sir Leonard Hutton, the first professional captain of England in a world vanished for ever: 'I saw Len Hutton in his prime| Another time| another time' (*Various Voices*: 35, 37, 168).[2]

Cricket reoccurs throughout Pinter's work. In his 1964, 1969 adaptations of L. P. Hartley's (1895–1972), novel *The Go-Between*, first published in 1953, set in the English countryside in the summer of 1900, a framing prologue and episodic technique interweaves the distant past with the present memories of an old man remembering. Subsequently, in the film the cricket match provides the foreground for messages, intrigue and betrayal. *Silence* (1968) is a short play that 'took a long time to write – longer in fact than any full-length play of mine' (cited Hayman, 1976: 82). In the words of Peter Hall (1930–), who directed at the National Theatre, many of Pinter's plays, it 'was a beautiful, heartbreaking evocation of the contradictions of memory'. Hall adds, 'I would think that the problems of what is true, what is false, are going to go on being an obsession with Pinter' (cited Batty, 2005: 165). It has three characters, two men and a woman. All are living in a world of memories. Rumsey is 'a man of forty' and 'Bates a man in his middle thirties' ([32]). In response to a question concerning the origins of the names Rumsey and Bates, Pinter responded that they opened the bowling for Hampshire and Sussex, 'but I did not consciously think of them when I was writing *Silence*. I simply looked in my mind for what I felt to be country names' (Letter to William Baker, 12 August 1971).

Alan Wilkinson in his 'Introduction' to *The Catch a Correspondence* (2003) co-authored with Pinter, speaks of their mutual 'passion for cricket'. Pinter 'has been associated with Gaieties Cricket Club – a wandering side – for over thirty years'. *The Catch* celebrates Pinter's love of cricket and memorialises a great 'catch off Ossie at Stokesley' many years previously. A fellow-member of the Gaities recalled, 'I've never seen a better catch at any level of cricket' ([7]). The correspondence reveals Pinter's encyclopaedic knowledge and memory of the game, its language, rituals and customs.

In his last question to Pinter, Wilkinson asked him, 'Did anyone "google"?' The reply was 'not a soul googled' ([16]). The question 'was inspired' according to Wilkinson 'by the last sentence of that provocative passage in *No Man's Land* [written in 1974] in which Spooner' – a name of another cricketer, a very fine batsman, as well as a person who utters Spoonerisms – 'interrogates Hirst about his wife'. She is associated with past beauty, 'How beautiful she was, how tender and how true' ([7]). Spooner then asks Hirst (a bowler who also played like Spooner in the pre-1914 period but for Yorkshire, Spooner on the other hand for the neighbouring county and traditional enemy, Lancashire) 'Tell me with what speed she swung in the air, with what velocity she came off the wicket, whether she was responsive to finger spin, whether you could bowl a shooter with her, or an off break with a leg break action. In other words, did she google?' (*No Man's Land*: 30). Essentially great cricketing moments are inextricably bound up with tremendous sexual fantasies and idyllic memories. Moreover, the two other characters in *No Man's Land*, Foster and Briggs, were also cricketers from the pre-1914 era. Foster a sparkling batsman for Warwickshire was left crippled in 1915 by a motorcycle accident. Briggs an all-rounder for Lancashire had epilepsy and died at the age of 30. Both are servants in the play!

It was through the Gaieties that Pinter met Arthur Wellard (1902–1980), who played for Somerset, England and then the Gaieties, finally becoming an Umpire. In a powerful prose tribute to Arthur Wellard first published in 1981, Pinter exhibits his knowledge and recall of the game. In spite of his years, Wellard is transformed into a hero. Pinter recalls Wellard, in the fading light, last man at the age of 72 winning a game in the final over 'the ball had gone miles, in the long-on area, over the boundary for four'. As an umpire, a judge,

'Arthur was strictly impartial by the highest standards.' A great hero to Pinter, he concludes his tribute, 'He gave me his England cap and the stump he knocked over when he bowled Badcock' (*VV*: 46–47, 51, 53). In Pinter's work, cricket terms and names reverberate with *double entendres*, as puns, as verbal games and are forever associated with idyllic days.

Friendships and Betrayals

Friendships too from school days remain with Pinter. These provide remarkable evidence of continuity and stability, as does cricket, in a world of fluidity and betrayal. Pinter himself admits to an early youthful betrayal. When he was 17 in 1947, he took a friend's girl-friend for a walk and sat down in the long grass with her. He knew this was wrong. Subsequently two of his friends, not the one he betrayed, invited Pinter for a walk. They went for a long walk, then walked into the middle of a desolate park. His friends then turned and left Pinter standing in the middle of the park. He felt extreme loneliness and guilt. The experience still haunts him (interview with Roberto Ando, 1998).

His work seethes with betrayals, especially in sexual and political matters. In the early one-act plays *The Room*, *The Dumb Waiter* and *A Slight Ache* (1958), the threat comes from the outside and pierces ordinary routines and rituals, the shields of words and repetitive actions. In *The Birthday Party*, Stanley retreats to shabby digs in a Sussex seaside town, Eastbourne, yet his presumed past catches up with him. In the later *Betrayal* (1978), a reverse time-sequencing with the conclusion at the beginning, serves to highlight the betrayal over many years of friends and husbands. A publisher's wife, a liter-ary agent and his best friend each in their own way betray one another. Theatrically, the drama reflects its author's own betrayal of his wife as he too was conducting a 7-year-long affair with the wife of a close friend.

Cinematically, Pinter's 1987–1988 adaptation of Fred Uhlman's novel *Reunion*, published in 1971, in the film of the same name, directed by the American Jerry Schatzberg (1927–), focuses on a return to a country after more than half a century. A successful ageing New Yorker returns to Germany from which he fled in the early 1930s. His father had fought proudly in the First World War as a medical officer for the country that subsequently turned around and brutally tormented his family, killing millions of his fellow Jews. The young boy's best friend appears to betray him, yet 'betrays' his own sister, family and 'country' by resisting the Reich and is executed in an abortive plot against Hitler.

In *The Homecoming* set in an old house in north London, a member of a family of taxi drivers and undefined nefarious occupations, returns from America with a new wife. By the end of the drama, the new wife, Ruth, has taken over control of the family, her husband is left mute, the others possess her when she wishes. A contemporary at school of Pinter's, Barry Supple (1930–) observes that 'at bottom' Pinter 'is fascinated by the concrete world of personal history'. For Supple 'a Pinter play is . . . a great echo-chamber in which the only sources of sound are the prosaic data of the dramatist's life history'. In that chamber 'nearly all the sounds are magnified and distorted into bizarre and sometimes shocking combinations' (*Jewish Chronicle*, 25 June 1965: 31). Such a revelation cemented a breach between Pinter and Supple – begun at the age of 16 when Pinter beat him on the running track – as if a betrayal, a personal betrayal, occurred. Incidentally, Supple went on from Hackney Downs to a glittering academic career as an economic historian. He became Professor of Economic History at Cambridge University and Master of St. Catherine's College, Cambridge.

Pinter has on the whole kept faith over the years with his friends formed during his school days. The most obvious example is the instance of the distinguished actor and academic Henry Woolf (1930–). Pinter dedicated *The Hothouse*, first written in the winter of 1958, to Woolf who as part of a postgraduate project at the University of Bristol Drama Department produced the initial Pinter production, *The Room* in May 1957 in which he also played the part of Mr. Kidd. Woolf played the part of the man, the only character in Pinter's *monologue* (1972–1973) and returned from Canada, where he taught for many years at the University of Saskatchewan, to perform the role in 2002 at the National Theatre's Platform. He also took a number of parts in a series of Pinter sketches. Two years earlier he had returned to play in the revival of *The Room* performed in 2000 with *Celebration*, written in 1999–2000, at the Almeida Theatre, Islington under Pinter's direction.

Woolf was in London again in July of 2007 when he appeared in a revival of *The Hothouse* at the National Theatre, Lyttleton stage. Woolf plays the part of the head porter Tubb. In a *Guardian* article, 'My Sixty Years in Harold's Gang', published 12 July 2007 Woolf remembers his school days during the last years of the war and just after. There was a group of six, the majority was Jewish, two were not, including the blond Ron Percival, the source for Pete in *The Dwarfs*. Pinter and Percival, Woolf recalls, were fierce rivals for girls. Another friend from those years was Michael (Mick) Goldstein who went to live in Australia and to whom Pinter dedicated *Other Places: Three Plays* (1982). Goldstein and Pinter did not go to the same school, however they and the others were all obsessive table-tennis players at the Hackney Boys' Club, and passionate about ideas and argument (cited *B*: 12, 16).

The guiding light for them was the Hackney Downs English Teacher Joseph Brearley (1909–1973) who told the group to focus first upon their own lives and worry later about a depressing world, one in which the holocaust had just occurred and atomic bombs had fallen upon Hiroshima and Nagasaki. None of the boys had any money but that did not stop them, walking for hours, endlessly talking, laughing, arguing and citing literature. Pinter was at the forefront in introducing the others to new authors such as Samuel Beckett (1906–1989), Henry Miller (1891–1980), John Dos Passos (1896–1970). In *monologue* first performed by Woolf in 1973, the only character echoes Woolf's reminiscences of his Hackney youth: 'Who was your best mate, who was your truest mate? You introduced me to Webster and Tourneur, admitted but who got you going on' the surrealists 'Tristan Tzara, Breton, Giacommetti and all that lot? Not to mention Louis-Ferdinand Celine, now out of favour.' Celine (1894–1961) was a French writer who collaborated with the Nazis and wrote extreme anti-semitic utterances. The Man in the *monologue* adds, 'And John Dos' ([4]), an illusion to John Dos Passos the American radical writer. Woolf remembers that Joe Brearley their teacher took them to see John Webster's revenge tragedy *The White Devil*. The drama had a profound impact, especially upon Pinter who more than half a century later still cites lines from it.

Henry Woolf remembers treachery and disloyalty, themes continually reverberating in Pinter's work. The whiff, the smell of betrayal, is implicit in Webster's play and in Woolf's memories. For Woolf, Pinter's loyalty to the mates of his youth remains paramount and friendship has taken on sacred qualities. This does not only apply to Harold Pinter's school gang. He remains, for instance, intensely loyal to the memory of his first agent, Emmanuel Wax ([1912]–1983), the publisher of *Landscape*, dedicating *No Man's Land* (1975) to him and movingly contributing to an anthology of reminiscences of *Jimmy* published in 1984, a year after his death. He also remains fiercely loyal to actors and actresses such as Jeremy Irons (1948–), Michael Gambon (1940–) and Penelope Wilton (1946–), who regularly appear in his work and participate in readings from them.

Post-War Years

There was by no means a safe world in spite of the war being over. In an interview with Lawrence M. Bensky published in the *Paris Review* (no. 39, Fall 1966), Pinter explains his observation that 'The world *is* a pretty violent place.' Pinter recalls:

> Everyone encounters violence in some way or other. It so happens I did encounter it in quite an extreme form after the war, in the East End, when the Fascists were coming back to life in England. I got into quite a few fights down there. If you looked remotely like a Jew you might be in trouble. Also, I went to a Jewish club, by an old railway arch, and there were quite a lot of people often waiting with broken milk bottles in a particular alley we used to walk through . . . .

> Another thing: we were often taken for Communists. If you went by, or happened to be passing, a Fascist's street meeting, and looked in any way antagonistic – this was in Ridley Road market, near Dalston Junction – they'd interpret your very being, especially if you had books under your arms, as evidence of your being a Communist. There was a good deal of violence there, in those days. (30–31)

The very fine novelist Alexander Baron's *With Hope, Farewell* published in 1952 tackles a similar subject: the war, its consequences, ethnicity, prejudice, a changing London. The life of the hero, a wartime fighter pilot, is traced. His personal confrontation with prejudice and identity historically reflects the re-emergence of anti-semitism in post-war London and especially the East End.

Pinter wrote on 31 January 1973 that he 'was too young to run into Mosley before the war'. However, he 'had a number of encounters with his boys in '46 and '47 in the Ridley Road area' of Dalston 'some of them very nasty' (letter to William Baker, 12 August 1971). At the time Pinter wore spectacles, sometimes he talked his way out of fights, sometimes he fought them. For Henry Woolf, Pinter and his other Jewish friends existed in their imaginations, leading a cerebral life that was seemingly safe. Similarly, Pinter's characters inhabit rooms reflecting their own private worlds. Juxtaposed with the cricket reminiscences, we see in this post-war world the extremes that make Pinter's work: a serene pastoral vision, and a jarring violence and destruction perpetually threatening, menacing.

Contributions to the School Magazine

At school, in addition to sporting, acting and the foundation of life-time friendships, Pinter contributed to the school magazine. His contributions are more than the fairly ordinary product of a highly intelligent and very sensitive schoolboy. They reveal literary influences and concerns, indicating the directions in which his future work is to take. Pinter's first published essay, a fine instance of his poetic prose – is written on the subject of 'James Joyce'. It appeared in the *Hackney Downs School Magazine,* Christmas 1946. For the youthful Pinter, *A Portrait of the Artist* is 'typical of Joyce, startlingly honest, true and forthright . . . a work of great lyrical beauty'. Of *Ulysses,* he writes:

> This enormous work, which depicts a day in the life of a Dubliner, stands supreme among twentieth-century literature. It is outstanding as a feat of narration, relating to streams of consciousness the innumerable thoughts that flit to and fro across the screen of the subconscious mind. Joyce omits nothing whatever, describing every thought, every word of this man. *Ulysses* is one of the most complete works of art

ever written . . . . Joyce has always had great feeling for words . . . no modern writer has used them to such effect.

And the description of *Finnegan's Wake* further pinpoints and anticipates Pinter's artistic development:

A nocturnal adventure, in which Joyce combined all languages to form an exquisite 'Joycean' prose. Here we are in a dream world, having as its main axis, the River Liffey, which flows through Dublin. All the rivers of the world meet it, and with them come all their past river-side connections. Great personalities are vaguely introduced, and beyond these runs the chatter of Irish charwomen washing clothes in the Liffey. Many fantastic characters appear . . .. Joyce stands out . . . as a very great humourist. At length the whole dream world falls asleep, and the words become drowsy and sleepy, and slowly the words subside into softness, softly drifting, and the work ends where it begins, in the middle of a sentence.

Pinter begins his schoolboy essay by exalting Joyce as the artist in exile who 'As a very sensitive young man . . . experienced seething discontent with his life in Dublin.' Pinter notes how Joyce 'rebelled against his narrow, catholic environment, his home, his religion and his country, and left Ireland to return but once. Even though he spent most of his life abroad, all his work was about Dublin, which was the one great influence of his life – a great Irish Catholic shadow that for ever lay over him'. Many autobiographical parallels connect the London poet with his admired Irish predecessor. Pinter still lives in London, but far from Hackney: his has been the voyage from Hackney to Chiswick, Worthing, Regent's Park, via Stratford-upon-Avon, and now the Campden Hill area.

Pinter's poem 'O Beloved Maiden', has not I think been republished, neither has the short essay 'Blood Sports', also published in the school magazine. In this the young Pinter writes with passion, opposing fox hunting and other such pursuits. The earliest dated poem, which so far Pinter has allowed to be published, is one dated 1948 called 'School Life'. This unusually long poem for Pinter – his poems become shorter, increasingly so, with age, has four verses and is as its title suggests, concerned with school life and with the introduction of a 'stranger'

either a new boy or teacher – as usual in Pinter's world, the exact nature
of the stranger is unspecified (*VV*: 115–116).

Pinter has acknowledged in prose and in poetry the debt to his
English Master, 'Joseph Brearley 1909–1977'. In his poem of that
name first published in *Collected Poems and Prose* in 1977 and subsequently reprinted in selections of Pinter's work and in the magazine
Soho Square he movingly recalls walks over London with 'Dear Joe'.
The poem concludes 'You're gone. I'm at your side, | Walking with
you from Clapton Pond to Finsbury Park, | And on, and on.' The
poem is replete with specific topographical references to the landscape of London, to 'Clapton Pond to Stamford Hill', to 'Manor
House to Finsbury Park', 'to Hackney Downs' and to 'the dead 653
trolleybus' (*VV*: 163). This is a characteristic feature of Pinter's work.
His drama is full of the specific place names of the great capital and
lists. Pinter loves his lists and plays with them brilliantly, illustrating
the adage from the sublime to the ridiculous.

Films

In addition to the sporting and writing activity at school, Pinter
actively took part in the school debating society. Of course attitudes and opinions expressed during school debates tend not to
reflect actual beliefs. The pleasure rests in arguing for the sake of
arguing, parrying sudden twists and turns, and expecting – usually
justifiable – to watch the others make fools of themselves: as characters in Pinter's plays do. In his final debate, Pinter seconded the
motion that 'In view of its progress in the last decades, the Film is
more promising in its future as an art form than the Theatre' (*Hackney Downs School Magazine*: no. 164 Spring 1948: 12). He clearly
took this proposition seriously, for a few months earlier, in the
autumn of 1947, he spoke to his schoolmates on 'Realism and
Post-Realism in the French Cinema' (no. 163: 13). Pinter's focus
was Marcel Carné's (1906–1996) *Les Enfants du Paradis*. This 1945
film centres on the relationship between art and life, fantasy and
reality. It captures the Pinteresque poetry of dreams on the edge of
destruction and chaos, the whiff of betrayal during the Nazi occupation of France (embodied, for instance, in the work and opinions
of Louis-Ferdinand Céline).

In an interview with Peter Florence (1964–) at the British Library held in 2004, Pinter recalled that when he was 14 he formed his own film society in Hackney with his friends. The film that had the most lasting impact upon his imagination was Salvador Dali (1904–1989) and Luis Buñuel's (1900–1983), 1924 silent film *Un Chien Andalou*. The image remaining in his mind, haunting his imagination, was that of the opening sequence with its juxtaposition of a man sharpening a straight razor and methodically slicing a women's eyeball down the middle. This is juxtaposed with the moon crossing the clouds. Pinter remembers the setting of a Parisian apartment, a window three stories up, traffic proceeding along the street and the attack on the woman by her lover. Other images in the film, surrealistic ones of a grand piano, donkeys, and escape by walking out onto a beach and the sea haunt Pinter. Moreover, Pinter reveals in his British Library interview with Peter Florence that the cinema was a stronger, more powerful, influence on him before actual theatrical performances were.

This influence may be seen in the fragmentary sequences interwoven with frequent cutting backwards and forwards between the present and the past in his work. In the film script adaptation of others' work such as L. P. Hartley's *The Go-Between* (1970), John Fowles' *The French Lieutenant's Woman* (1981) and, to take one other instance from Pinter's screenplays, Uhlman's *Reunion* (1989), one shot gives way to another, time past becomes time present as in the un-filmed script of Marcel Proust's great novel *À la Recherché du Temps Perdu* that Pinter worked on intermittently during the 1970's. In Pinter's *Betrayal* too images of the past, reverse chronologies and memory, interweave with the present.

Pinter's experience of movies and their impact upon him is reflected in the sense of violence and gratuitous sex found in his work. Characters in *Old Times* (1971) make references to the *Odd Man Out*, a 1947 film that established Carol Reed (1906–1976) as a major director. Adapted by R. C. Sherriff (1896–1976), author of the powerful First World War drama *Journey's End* (1930), from a novel by F. L. Green (1902–1953), a Belfast schoolmaster, James Mason (1909–1984), played the role of a haunted IRA gunman in an unnamed city, in fact Belfast. The film created a powerful cinematic impression of the gunman's final hours, and was nominated for an Oscar. Betrayal and desperation play out against a bleak urban landscape. There are memorable performances from Robert Newton (1905–1956) and Cyril Cusack (1910–1993) who played the part of Sam in *The Homecoming*. Images of being hunted down, cornered and captured are very prevalent in Pinter's work.

They owe much to his film experiences in the 1940s as well as personal ones. Personally, as noted, he was no coward standing up to fascists. He too detested bullies. Henry Woolf recalls how Pinter stood up to a teacher at school named De la Feld who was over 6 feet tall and took personal pleasure in humiliating boys by pulling their hair or hitting their bare legs with a ruler. At the age of 15, Pinter refused to take anymore lessons from him and personally went to the headmaster to complain (cited Woolf, the *Guardian*, 12 July 2007: 25).

Shakespeare at School

At school, encouraged by Joe Brearley, Pinter took a dominating role in two Brearley theatrical productions: *Macbeth* in the summer of 1947 and *Romeo and Juliet* in the following summer. The *Hackney Downs School Magazine*, Summer 1947 (no. 162) critic commented on Pinter's performance as Macbeth which he played dressed in the khaki uniform of a post-Second World War British soldier serving in the Tropics, or even Palestine: 'Word-perfect, full-voiced, Pinter took the tragic hero through all stages of temptation, hesitation, concentration, damnation. He gave us both Macbeth's conflicts, inner and outer, mental and military, with vigour, insight and remarkable acting resource.' (12) The school reviewer was far more reserved about Pinter's performance as Romeo. Pinter 'flung himself on the floor of the Friars cell in passionate histrionic abandon'. However, he seemed to lack the vocal abilities 'needed to bring out all the subtle cadences of the poetry' (Summer 1948, no. 165: 18).

Girls

Pinter's Juliet was his school 'friend' Ron Percival with whom he was competing for girls. Rivalry, jealousy and conflict are associated with Pinter's early encounters with girls and associated with highly charged sexual experiences among the wartime blackouts and the dim lights.

Meetings in the dark with girls were part of life at the time. In his interview with Roberto Ando, Pinter remembers in particular at the age of 14 a particular encounter when he shared a Morison shelter, a reinforced inverted table, with the girl next door, the neighbour's daughter, during an air raid. The experience Pinter remembered for the rest of his life. He didn't want the all clear to sound, the destructive air raid to conclude. Pinter's first experience of writing is associated too with the opposite sex. He really started to write at the age of 13 when he was madly infatuated with a girl. In despair and jealousy, she tormented him, led him rather a dance. Deeply jealous, young and fervent, he began writing out of rejected love. In fact, Pinter was in love with language, drunk with language and intoxicated with language for its own sake. Dylan Thomas' (1914–1953) poetry in particular appealed; the sense was not important, what was important for the young Pinter was the pure sound.

End of School Days

In spite of insecurities reflected, for instance, in a poem 'School life' (1948), Pinter's time at Hackney Downs was not unhappy and certainly formative. He left school in July 1948. He had considered applying for Oxford and Cambridge, where contemporaries such as Barry Supple went, but Pinter didn't have the Latin required for admission at the time. Pinter's vision of Oxford existence in any case was hardly an academic one. It 'was all dreaming spires, sunlit quads and girls with milk-white thighs' (cited *B*: 20). Encouraged by Joe Brearley, he applied for admission to RADA, the Royal Academy of Dramatic Arts. The assessor for the London County Council, R. D. Smith (1914–1985), subsequently to play an important role in Pinter's professional life, recommended Pinter for a grant. Pinter started at RADA in the autumn of 1948, just before his eighteenth birthday.

Chapter Two
Ireland, Precarious Existence and Marriage

RADA

RADA was a disaster and the years after school were exceedingly insecure ones. According to Pinter's 'Profile: Playwright on his own' published in *The Observer*, 15 September 1963, he 'faked a nervous breakdown and, unknown to his parents, trampled the streets for months while continuing to draw a grant' (13), probably gathering and absorbing material for the tape-recorder-like imitation of speech patterns found in his subsequent plays. He actually, although erratically, attended classes at RADA during the Autumn of 1948 and Spring of 1949. In the unpublished and autobiographical prose account of these years written during his early twenties, entitled *The Queen of all the Fairies*, Pinter observes, 'When I went to Acting School I lost no contact with my friends.' He was not disloyal to his Hackney gang. He 'couldn't bear' RADA as it was, 'full of poofs and ponces, upstairs and downstairs, suspendered beauties, darlings and darlinged, "shop" and flourish'. He adds that 'the instructors were mostly crap too'. An instructor, he 'hated . . . and she reported me as insolent, ill-mannered and turbulent'. So he 'faked a nervous break-down and attended no more', noting that as his very close friend from Hackney schooldays, who became a university professor of English in Canada, Morris Wernick, 'called it, my poncing days began; from café to pisshole and back' (cited *B*: 20–21). The day Pinter left RADA after a final interview with its head, he met three friends from Hackney. They took a bus to Lords. Pinter remembers 'the green turf stretched out in the afternoon sun [and that] a late cut sent the ball skimming towards them'. He adds, 'it was one of the happiest days of my life' (cited *Pinter in the Theatre*: 18–19).

Pinter was leading a double life. Living at home, he would leave at a regular time, giving his parents the impression he was going to RADA, but really to the Hackney Library and then wait for his friends to come out of school to tramp the streets with them. Hackney and the neighbouring Whitechapel Library, Aldgate East, became a sanctuary and a university for Pinter and others. Bernard Kops in a poem written in a vain attempt to prevent the closure of the Aldgate East, Whitechapel library branch, in 2000, writes of how the library provided an escape, a refuge. In 'The reference library, where my thoughts were to rage.| I ate book after book, page after page' (*Bernard Kops' East End*: 8).

Conscientious Objector

On 10 October 1948, Pinter turned 18 and was eligible for the then compulsory National Service. All able-bodied young men of 18 had to spend 2 years in the armed forces. Morris Wernick served in the Roger Artillery, Henry Woolf in the Royal Air Force. Pinter on the other hand became a conscientious objector, refusing to serve. He was not a pacifist, and is adamant that if he had been slightly older he would have served either as a volunteer or a conscript in the war against Hitler and Fascism. Called before a tribunal after spending a night in a prison cell, he said that he 'disapproved of the Cold War and wasn't going to help it along as' an 18-year-old. This was not enough to convince the tribunal and following subsequent trials, Pinter was fined twice, for those days fairly large sums. These were paid by Pinter's father who was forced to borrow the money to pay them. Pinter fully expected to be imprisoned and took his 'toothbrush to the trials' (cited *Pinter in the Theatre*: 18–19). Such an act was brave, if expensive for his father. Pinter was lucky not to be jailed. Harold Hobson wrote in the *Sunday Times* on 25 May 1958, the only real positive review of *The Birthday Party*. Hobson observed: 'Mr. Pinter has got hold of a primary fact of existence. We live on the verge of disaster' (11). In the late 1940s and 1950s, Britain and the West were in the grip of the Cold War with the Soviet Union and

Pinter's personal future, as a drama school dropout, was also very uncertain in uncertain times.

1949–1951

W. S. Graham

During the years 1949–1951, Pinter used his parent's home as a base, explored London, wandered, wrote and read. In 1949, for instance, he discovered the work of Scottish born poet William Sydney Graham (1918–1986), who settled in St. Ives in Cornwall. At the Ilkley Literature Festival in 1994, Pinter said, 'I first read his poetry in 1949, that's a bloody long time ago now. I was 20.' Pinter 'found his language magical', adding that 'when you have a unique sense of language like Graham or Shakespeare, you come across a line which hits you midships and sends you all a flutter.' Pinter is unaware of any 'other poet who can move through about three lines and come out the fourth in one breath'. Graham is 'dealing with such delicate potentials – silence and the other side of language'. Pause and silence punctuate Pinter's own work. Both Pinter and Graham's writings are, to adopt Pinter's words, 'ravished by language and the conundrum of language'. Both are obsessed with the ambiguity of words (www.haroldpinter.org).

Shakespeare

Shakespeare too remains a source of great inspiration for Pinter. 'A Note on Shakespeare' is a prose essay first published in *Granta* (Autumn 1993) and reprinted in *Various Voices* (2005) where it is dated 1950. The distinguished critic and former BBC producer Martin Esslin (1918–2002) in his early influential study of Pinter draws upon material in 'A Note on Shakespeare' for his title and central arguments. In *The Peopled Wound: The Work of Harold Pinter* (1970), Esslin stresses the fundamental ambiguity of Pinter's dramatic universe. For Esslin, interpretation of Pinter's drama will be essentially elusive. In 'A Note on Shakespeare' the young Pinter observes that 'Shakespeare writes of the open wound and, through him, we know it open and know it closed.' Shakespeare too is essentially ambiguous: 'In attempting to approach Shakespeare's work in its entirety, you are called upon to grapple with a perspective in which the horizon alternately collapses and re-forms behind you.'

The final seven paragraphs of Pinter's fourteen-paragraph note consists of increasingly lengthy listings of Shakespearean characteristics, cumulative pronouns, similar to lists frequently found in Pinter's later drama. Shakespeare 'aborts, he meanders, he loses his track, he overshoots his mark and he drops his glasses'. Pinter's essay ends with a single short paragraph of antithesis. There are three short staccato sentences: 'The fabric never breaks. The wound is open. The wound is peopled' (*VV*: 5–7). His essay is replete with dense, swirling metaphors, grounded in everyday existence yet forcing their reader to create fresh connections between known, understood vocabulary and unusual, disturbing ideas. There is even a bullying, nagging, threatening perspective implicit in the repetitions. 'A Note on Shakespeare' has then many of the qualities found in Pinter's best writing.

Kullus

Such qualities are found too in the prose poem named 'Kullus.' This was written in 1949 while Pinter lived at home and was first published in *Poems* (1968). There are three sections and we are in the familiar Pinter terrain of a room, space, a fight for its possession, a triangular relationship between two men and a woman. The exact nature of their relationships, past and present essentially are ambiguous. Power is shifting continually. In the initial movement or section, the speaker admits someone into his space, his territory, his room, Kullus. The intruder begins to criticise what he finds. He introduces someone with him, a girl wrapped in a shawl and they move onto the inhabitants' bed. The room has been occupied by other figures, conquered, colonised. In the second movement, the original occupant and the girl are taken over, controlled by Kullus. A further power shift takes place with the girl dominating the two men. By the cyclical conclusion, the host reasserts control. Here are Pinter's continual preoccupations: ambiguity, shifting human relationships; the conflict for power and control of others, of space, of a room.

Early Poems

Pinter's first published work, apart from those poems and prose pieces that appeared in his school magazine, belong to this period. 'New Year in the Midlands' and 'Chandeliers and Shadows' appeared in *Poetry London*, in the August 1950 issue. Started by J. M. Tambimuttu (1915–1983), the Tamil poet, editor and critic, in 1939, the magazine ran until the Summer issue of 1951. Pinter's poem 'One a Story, Two a Death' appeared in the final issue. His poem 'I Shall Tear off my Terrible Cap' was published in *Poetry Quarterly* also in the summer of 1951. They were attributed to 'Harold Pinta', a name Pinter occasionally used for his poetry during these years. The setting of 'New Year in the Midlands' is a rowdy pub around Christmas time. Pinter managed to pickup acting work for a short while appearing in the Christmas pantomime in Chesterfield. In the poem, there is a landlady who lumps 'Fellows between board', actors in shabby digs. We have a 'queer', and the 'crawling brass whores' with the 'clamping | Red-shirted boy' who is 'thudding his cage' with the women. While 'well-rolled' sailors who have been robbed when drunk are 'soon rocked to sleep'. The speaker of the poem (Pinter) becomes more drunk and more intimate with the landlady: who is described as 'the wansome lady'. Little detail is omitted in this realistic scene from the 'can of chockfull stuff', beer, to the brand name 'Whitbread Ale' or the fumbling 'luminous hands' of the drinkers as they 'Unpin the town's genitals' about to urinate or fornicate.

In 'New Year' the singing of 'O Celestial Light' alludes, ironically, to the return of the Messiah and the homosexual with 'pale | Deliberate eyes' is named after the New Testament Luke. The poem is replete with run-on lines, alliteration and internal rhymes. The poem contains a profusion of 'I' sounds preparing and continuing the echo of the word 'Luke'. Pinter cleverly uses a trochaic rhythm in, for instance, the line 'Straddled, exile always in one Whitbread Ale town' (*VV*: 119–120). There is here a sense of isolation and loneliness forcing the reader to ask the question: what is Pinter, the young man from Hackney, East London, doing in the Midlands town in the first place at Christmas time?

An interesting family story is associated with the poem serving to illustrate family pride and differing perspectives. Pinter remembers that 'There was only one member of [his] family' who seemed to be affluent. That was his 'great-Uncle Coleman who was in "business"' of one sort or another. 'He always wore felt carpet slippers and skull-cap at home, and was a very courteous man.' Pinter's 'father proposed that I show Uncle Coleman my poem in *Poetry London*.' Pinter reluctantly agreed to show 'New Year in the Midlands'. It 'was to do with a young actor's vagabond life in rep. It was heavily influenced by Dylan Thomas'. Pinter then quotes the lines: 'This is the shine, the powder and blood and here am I, | Straddled, exile always in one Whitbread Ale town, | Or such'. Pinter and his father 'sat in the room in silence while Uncle Coleman read this poem. When he reached those lines he stopped, looked over the magazine at us and said, "Whitbread shares are doing very well at the moment. Take my tip."' (cited *B*: 30)

During 1950, Pinter was also occasionally picking up BBC work. Late in 1950, he was in a sequence of R. D. Smith radio productions and played the small part of Abergavenny in Shakespeare's *Henry VIII*. Pinter's poetry brought in practically no money. Living at home and working as an occasional radio-actor, he decided to return to drama school. From January to July 1951, Pinter was at the Central School of Speech and Drama for two terms. Pinter was happier at the Central School than at RADA. He fell under the spell of Cicely Berry (1926–), a brilliant voice coach, and Stephen Joseph who subsequently created the Stoke-on-Trent and Scarborough theatres in the round, and other innovative theatrical ventures. Pinter also met Barry Foster (1927–2002), a fellow student and actor who was to remain a friend. Foster recalls the many faceted sides of Pinter's personality. On the one hand, Pinter could be very sociable and convivial, a great drinker and womaniser; on the other hand, highly estranged and morose.

In his poem 'I Shall tear off my Terrible Cap' published in C. Wrey Gardiner's (1901–1981), the poet, editor and publisher's *Poetry Quarterly* (Summer 1951), under the name 'Harold Pinta', the poet writes 'All spirits shall haunt me and all devils drink me;| O despite their dark drugs and the digs that they rib me; | I'll tear off my terrible cap' (*VV*: 126). Similar sentiments of desperation are found in 'Chandeliers and Shadows', published a year earlier in August 1950 in *Poetry London*. This has an epigraph from John

Webster's *The Duchess of Malfi* – 'I'll goe hunt the badger by owle-light: tis a deed of darknesse' – lines no doubt Joe Brearley introduced his pupil Pinter to. The poem conveys a scene of decadence and sexual depravity. Chaos predominates: 'worlds dying, suns in delirium', the universe, in this instance a room, is ruled over by a 'lunatic' and a 'locust' God. The universe is reduced to a decaying stage setting, an illusion reinforced at the end of the poem by an overt reference to *Twelfth Night*. Shakespeare's comedy and the conclusion of the Christmas festivities coalesce in a frightening vision. In this the room is not a place of refuge but one, with its 'gilded gondolas' being destroyed by 'the long betrayed monster' (God?).

The initial stanza is replete with images of rot and decay powerfully evoked by the use of internal line balance, for instance, 'In this brothel, in this room', 'the horsefly, the palsied stomacher'. Alliterative usage is particularly effective in the second and final stanza, reinforcing the overall sense of decay: there is crust, crumpled, camphor, stifle, split, splintered. The 'r' sounds, especially at the conclusion of the lines, creates a perception of destruction through the ripping and tearing of things, of the very universe itself (*VV*: 123–124).

A similar sense of isolation and decay is found in the unpublished, early autobiographical prose work 'Queen of All the Fairies' containing memories of Pinter's Hackney youth. He writes about his relationships, his friends, politics and 'emerges as an impassioned outsider and obstinate nonconformist who, even if the world is going to hell in a hand-cart, is determined to cling on to his freedom and independence of thought' (*B*: 33).

During this period Pinter was passionately involved with the actress Dilys Hamlett (1928–2002) then studying at the Old Vic Drama School. She recalls 'I always have an image of Harold striding down the street in his navy-blue coat with a rage against the world. But it was also a rage for life, a rage to do something, a rage to achieve something.' He also 'had a strong, possessive streak' (cited *B*: 35–36). Hamlett met someone else whom she subsequently married. Pinter was deeply hurt, and the memories of their relationship and activities resurface in his powerful drama *Old Times*.

Ireland

In the early summer of 1951, Pinter was forced to face reality. He had to find a job and successfully responded to an ad. in *The Stage*. He wrote to R. D. Smith, his BBC supporter, on 28 August 1951: 'I'm going . . . for a six-month tour in Shakespeare to Ireland next month' with the great Irish actor–manager Anew McMaster. 'I'm playing among others, Horatio, Bassanio and Cassio in *Othello*' (cited *B*: 36). The tour lasted from September 1951 until early 1953. Born in 1891 and dying in 1962, McMaster ('Mac') was in the Victorian actor–manager mould. Four years after his death, Pinter wrote a glowing tribute in *Mac*. For Pinter, '[Mac] was a realist. But he possessed a true liberality of spirit. He was humble . . ... He was a very great piss-taker.' This is very characteristic of Pinter. His memories are interlaced with the serious and the humorous, he doesn't forget the humanity of his subject. Pinter uses words from W. B. Yeats's 'Lapis Lazuli' to describe the essence of McMaster's acting and his personality: 'They know that Hamlet and Lear are gay,| Gaiety trans-figuring all that dread.' Pinter's description of Mac as Lear – 'At the centre of his performance was a terrible loss, desolation, silence' – is not only very moving but reaches into the depths of Pinter's own art and vision.

From this experience, Pinter learnt much about stagecraft, directing and acting. He writes in *Mac*, 'Ireland wasn't golden always, but it was golden sometimes and in 1950 [Pinter's error for 1951–1953] it was, all in all, a golden age for me and for others' (*VV*: 34, 32–33). In addition to performing in many diverse roles with McMaster, Pinter acted with the very fine actor Barry Foster and eventually played the leads with the superb, beautiful Irish actress Pauline Flanagan (1925–2003). She played Portia to Pinter's Bassanio, Mrs. Erylynne to his Lord Windermere, Gwendolen to Pinter's Jack Worthing. They fell in love and Pinter took her to London to meet his parents and his close friends. She remembers his passion for Yeats, especially his late poems and his frequent recitations from Eliot's *The Waste Land*. In London, Pinter took her to see films by Buñuel and the Marx Brothers. Pinter's mother was unhappy about the relationship with Pauline, an Irish-Catholic. Their economic futures were not bright, and they separated although remaining on good terms (*B*: 39–40). In 1976 Pinter directed her in the Broadway production of William Archibald's (1917–1970), *The Innocents* (1950), based on Henry James's 'The Turn of the Screw' (1898).

In Ireland, Pinter continued to write poetry. 'The Islands of Aran Seen from the Moher Cliffs' (1951), in five verse quatrains, celebrates the beauty, the grandeur, the power of the coastal scenery and the for ever present mythology associated with that part of Ireland. These are rural rather than urban poems. The railings and landscape of Hackney are replaced by that of the Irish coastal countryside. There are also poems of loss, of deprivation, isolation, alienation, betrayal and love. These are all motifs to reoccur frequently in Pinter's writing. 'Episode', dated 1951 is a poetic dialogue with a rejected main voice, an apparently successful rival, the 'He' and a silent 'She' over whom the two are feuding. The speaker asks in the first section 'Why do you follow?' then 'Why do you leave me?' and 'Why do you stay with me?' In the third and last section, the sequence of these questions is changed: 'Why did you leave me?' then 'Why did you follow?' with the final assertion 'I am her stranger.' This is the world of the later *Landscape* and *Betrayal*.

There are also poems of celebration. For instance, 'Poem' (1953) speaks of love and stability. The four stanzas of six lines each, open 'I walked one morning with my only wife.' The last four words are repeated through the poem that ends on a note of Pinteresque ambiguity set among the Irish coastal scenery: 'We parted ways on the sunlit hill, | She silent, I to the farther west' (*VV*: 131, 134, 143). Speaking in 1994 at the Dublin Gate Theatre Pinter Festival, Harry White, conveys the essence of what Ireland means and meant to Pinter. 'Ireland symbolises the past and is an agent of romantic or nostalgic recollection or it embodies and encodes the threat of violence.' (cited *B*: 43)

In the Ireland of the early 1950s, Pinter learnt real stagecraft, fell yet again in love, experienced the beauty of rural as opposed to urban landscapes, wrote and discovered Samuel Beckett with whom he subsequently formed a close friendship. Pinter recalls that 'One day I came across, I stumbled across, a poetry magazine called *Poetry Ireland* edited by David Marcus in which I found a fragment of Beckett's *Watt*. I was stunned by it.' Unable to find a copy, he removed it from

Battersea Public Reserve Library. In a conversation at the Royal Court Theatre in October 2005, Pinter confessed to his only criminal act. In 1951 he took out Samuel Beckett's *Murphy* last borrowed in the year of its publication, 1938. He kept the book which he still has and it is very precious to him. Pinter avidly read Beckett's tale of a solipsistic hero existing in a condemned structure in London's West Brompton. His only relief is to remove his clothes and strapped to a rocking-chair rocks himself into a non-conscious state. His girlfriend Celia forces him into an insane asylum. Murphy finds the treatment of restoration to the external world repulsive. A rocking-chair is a major symbol in Pinter's first performed dramatic work, *The Room* (1957). A good deal of Pinter's work contains an examination of the conflict between being alone and being part of society.

Pinter recalls of his reading of *Murphy* 'I suddenly felt that what his writing was doing was walking through a mirror into the other side of the world which was, in fact, the real world. What I seemed to be confronted with was a writer inhabiting his innermost self.' This intense self-reflection is combined with humour. 'The book was also very funny. I never forgot the laughs I immediately got from reading Beckett.' Pinter continues, 'But what impressed me was something about the quick of the world. It was Beckett's own world, but had so many references to the world we actually share' (cited *B*: 43). So by the time he left Mac's repertory company to face the realities of the world of London, the foundations of Pinter's stage-craft, professionalism and creative sensibilities had been formed and shaped by formative, personal, theatrical and literary experience.

1953–1957

The period following Pinter's return from Ireland early in 1953 to until 1957 was spent writing and attempting to earn a living. Early in 1953 for a 3-month period, Pinter had a 3-month contract with Donald Wolfit's (1902–1968) company at the King's Theatre Hammersmith. Pinter was too independent for the dictatorial Wolfit, although he learnt a good deal of theatrical craft from him, as he learnt from that other great actor–manager, Anew McMaster. Pinter's contract with Wolfit wasn't renewed.

The late spring of 1953 until the summer of 1954 saw Pinter in a series of roles and odd jobs. He returned briefly to Mac's company for a role in an adaptation of Bertolt Brecht's *The Mother* (1930–1931) at the Embassy Theatre, Swiss Cottage, and picked up radio work. In addition to writing, Pinter had various odd jobs ranging from a dishwasher, a door-to-door salesman, a bouncer at the Astoria Dance Hall, Charing Cross Road, a doorman, a hawker in Oxford Street, a waiter, a snow shoveller. At nights he usually returned to the parental home in Thistlewaite Road. He drew upon his experiences in his writing. His plays are replete with London topographical and other local knowledge. In the late play *Celebration*, Pinter draws upon his earlier experiences. In this play, a waiter beguiles his fantastically wealthy diners with stories and aesthetic allusions. Pinter worked as a waiter at the National Liberal Club. He was fired for engaging a member in lengthy discussions on poetry!

Pinter had few illusions about the theatre. Henry Woolf wrote to Pinter when he was in rep. with Mac's company in Ireland, saying that he wished to become an actor. Pinter responded in characteristically blunt, down to earth language: 'What do you want to go into this shit-house for? This shit-house of a profession.' Pinter added, 'You'll meet very few people you want to have a drink with. It can be gold and diamonds but there's also bags of the other stuff.' Perhaps here the physically handsome Pinter is alluding to the fact that he was constantly experiencing close physical relationships with a string of highly attractive actresses and ladies working, for instance, as assistant stage managers. In other words, to use a London expression, he was 'pulling the birds!' The assault upon former butchers in *The Homecoming* is probably Pinter's revenge for the butcher who had the assistant stage manager in Whitby fired following a fling with Pinter in June 1954.

In the early months of 1954, Pinter changed his stage name to David Baron. The response from R. D. Smith, Pinter's BBC mentor, was 'I think you must be mad to change your name from Harold Pinter to David Baron . . . What a name to call yourself!' (cited *B*: [45], 47). Following Whitby and despite its theatre manager's threat of permanent theatrical unemployment, Pinter then toured in a L. du Garde Peach's (1890–1974) farce manipulating the ears of a dummy horse. During this run, Pinter stayed in shabby digs in

Eastbourne, subsequently to be theatrically immortalised in *The Birthday Party*.

During the winter season of 1954, Pinter performed in various plays at the Huddersfield Rep. He performed at the Colchester Rep. for most of 1955, where he had a relationship with Jill Johnson. During a late June engagement with the company in Port Stewart, Co. Londonderry, Pinter stayed with Jill and the visiting Mick Goldstein, a friend from Hackney days. Pinter dedicated *Other Places: Three Plays*, *Other Places: Four Plays* (1984) and *Poems* (1968, 1971) to him. From them, he learnt that Peter Hall, later to direct much Pinter, was going to direct at the Arts Theatre, Samuel Beckett's *Waiting for Godot*. Pinter and Jill managed to see a performance. So even though Pinter was performing in provincial rep., in traditional plays, he was still creatively producing and involved with avant-garde artistic developments.

March to September 1956 was spent with the Barry O'Brien Company at the Palace Court, Bournemouth. From October 1956 to March 1957 Pinter was at the Alexandra Theatre, Birmingham, the Intimate Theatre, Palmer's Green, North London, and then the Connaught Theatre, Worthing where he also watched a lot of cricket. He played villains and the leading-men in Agatha Christie (1890–1976), for instance, in her *Witness for the Prosecution* ([1925]). He took on the role of the mad killer in the Vosper–Christie who-done-it *Love from a Stranger*. All of course a far cry from *Waiting for Godot* ([1953])! All the while, Pinter was learning stage techniques which reappear in his subsequent work. Mary Hayley Bell's (1911–2005), *The Uninvited Guest* (1953) contains a key interrogation scene in which Pinter appeared in Colchester in April 1955. An escaped mental patient performed by Pinter has his back to the audience. He is fiercely questioned by the other characters. This kind of scene is also found in *The Birthday Party*.

At the Palace Court Theatre, Bournemouth, Pinter met Guy Vaesen (1912–2002) who was the production director and company manager at the Palace Court. He took Pinter under his wing, forming a lifelong friendship. They subsequently worked together at the Connaught Theatre, Worthing. A talented artist and screen printer, Vaesen illustrated the first edition of *Family Voices* (1981) and co-directed *The Lover* (1962) at the New Arts Theatre in September

1963, directed the radio-play *Night School* in September 1966. In May 1969 Vaesen adapted from the Pinter's 1962 screenplay a short-ened radio version of Robin Maugham's (1916–1981) short novel first published in 1948, *The Servant*. Vaesen directed in April 1968 on the BBC Radio Third Programme, *Landscape*. He also produced in August 1970 a recording of *Silence*. A projected sound adaptation of Pinter's screenplay, first written in 1970, from Aidan Higgins (1927–) 1966 novel *Langrishe Go Down* for the thirtieth anniversary of Radio 3 due to be broadcast on 18 June 1976, was blocked. The American owner of the rights refused permission. Vaesen also produced the 1975 radio production of *monologue*.

Vivien Merchant

Also in the Bournemouth Company was the actress Ada Thomson who used the stage name of Vivien (she admired Vivien Leigh [1913–1967]) and Merchant (a brother was a merchant sailor). Vivien Merchant (1929–1982) grew up in Manchester. Educated at a convent school, she went on stage at the age of 14. She was in Wolfit's Company at the same time as Pinter at the King's Theatre, Hammersmith early in 1953. Then apparently the sparks didn't fly between them. At Bournemouth she was *the* leading lady: sensuous, flexible and with long, luscious legs. Pinter subsequently utilised her alluring physical presence and sexual power in his early plays and films. Theirs was a tempestuous relationship. Vaesen recalls, 'After about six weeks of the season . . . Vivien knocked on my door and said "Is *he* going to stay in the company?"' Vaesen replied, '"Yes." She responded "Well, if he doesn't go, I shall have to leave. I can't act with him." And so she left.' She returned.

In any case, she and Pinter married in a Bournemouth registry office on 14 September 1956. Pinter's parents Jack and Frances honeymooned in Bournemouth. Pinter, forever rebellious, recalls, 'I just married her [Vivien] and that was that, really. I made a booking at the Registry Office but what I'd forgotten, and which Vivien certainly didn't know, is that it was Yom Kippur', the most sacred day in the Jewish calendar, a day of prayer, reflection and fasting. 'I rang my parents to tell them I was getting married, and there was quite a bit of perturbation and dismay: not only was I getting married out of the Jewish faith, but I had accidentally chosen Yom Kippur, which seemed an insult to my parents. But that was it, really . . .. I had to live with that.' Although Pinter denies it, the seeds for *The Homecoming* have their roots in his first marriage. In the play, an East End family comes to terms with a *shiksa* (a non-Jewess) who enters into their house, having married one of their sons. Eventually, she takes over, gaining dominance and control. Pinter remembers 'When we met, she [Vivien] was the star. She really was. She was a star in rep.' (cited *B*: 53–54).

Following a short Cornish honeymoon, they performed for 6 months in rep. at Torquay. Vivien played the leading roles, Pinter the lesser ones, although he did play a prominent part in *Separate Tables* (1954) by Terence Rattigan (1911–1977), a dramatist whom he subsequently came to admire for his sense of understatement, stagecraft and depiction of the conflict between people.

The Dwarfs

All the while, Pinter was writing. In addition to poems, a novel and short stories belong to this period. *The Dwarfs* was started around 1952 and completed in 1956. Henry Woolf in his 'My 60 Years in Harold's gang', views *The Dwarfs* as very revealing of the early and adolescent Hackney years (24–25). *The Dwarfs* well indicates central motifs to be found throughout Pinter's work: memories, whether real or imagined, and that occur at the most unexpected moments; male friendships, bonds and memories of these associations; guilt, loyalty and betrayal; the significance of the seemingly insignificant. In the words of Joan Bakewell (1933–), with whom Pinter was to conduct a lengthy 7-year affair, the foundation for the powerful play and film *Betrayal*, Pinter 'doesn't need to do much more than walk to the tube – that is full of significance for him' (cited *B*: 60). People's perceptions of rooms of one shape or another dominate *The Dwarfs* as they do Pinter's other work. Similarly, the politics between people, the conscious or unconscious struggle for dominance, power and possession between them, reverberates throughout *The Dwarfs*. Moreover, it is replete with non sequiturs, puns, interrogative questions, staccato utterances, references to London, to art, to Bach, to Shakespeare, to T. S. Eliot, swiftly moving from the sublime to the ridiculous, from Shakespearean tragedy to the music hall.

Early Short Stories

To this period belong the short stories *The Black and White* and *The Examination;* the former was initially published in *Flourish*, the 'Royal Shakespeare Club Newspaper' in the summer of 1965 and reprinted a year later in the *Transatlantic Review*. *The Examination*, written in 1955, appeared in *Prospect*, in the summer of 1959, edited by Elaine Feinstein (1930–), then at Cambridge; it was reprinted in 1961 in *Encounter*. *The Black and White*, written between 1954 and 1955, was transformed in1959 by Pinter into a review sketch. Both echo using memory, the topography of London, in *The Black and White*, for instance, the 294 bus route (bus routes frequently reoccur in Pinter's work) from Marble Arch to Fleet Street. Both are characterised by reminiscences, short sentences, the language of London: 'I saw the last 296. It must have been the last. It didn't look like an all-night bus, in daylight' (*VV*: 87). Here we have the typical Pinteresque techniques of repetition, humour and irony.

In *The Examination* the Kullus figure occurs once again – it initially appeared in a prose poem of the same name from 1949. In a *Paris Review* 1966 interview, Pinter reflects that his 'ideas of violence carried on from' *The Examination*. He continues, 'That short story dealt very explicitly with two people in one room having a battle of an unspecified nature' concerning dominance. 'A threat is constant there; it's got to do with this question of being in the uppermost position, or attempting to be.' This is the reason why Pinter, for instance, was 'attracted' to Robin Maugham's 1948 novel *The Servant*, which Pinter rewrote in 1962 for the cinema: 'I wouldn't call this violence so much as a battle for positions, it's a very common, everyday thing.' Pinter also told his interviewer Lawrence M. Bensky 'the world *is* a pretty violent place, it's as simple as that' (30–31).

Chapter Three
Early Plays

The Room

It is uncertain when exactly Pinter began to write plays. Even when they become his dominant form, he continued to write poetry and short prose pieces. During the autumn of 1956, his old chum Henry Woolf was at the University of Bristol's Drama Department studying on a postgraduate year. Auriol Smith, the actor and producer, at the time was also studying in the department, looking for one-act plays and asked Woolf if he knew anybody who wrote them. Woolf wrote to his old friend Pinter about developing an idea they already had tossed about: a short play revolving around the image of two men fighting for dominance in a room. Newly married, Pinter was performing in Rattigan's *Separate Tables*, in Torquay. Pinter wrote *The Room* during a period of four afternoons and following his own rep. performances. The play directed by Henry Woolf was first performed at the Bristol University Drama Department on 15 and 16 May 1957. According to Woolf, the production 'cost four and six pence'. They had no money. Bert wasn't given, except for one performance, 'real bacon and eggs'. Moreover, the play Woolf recalls 'went down very well. It was menacing and very funny' (cited *B*: 67).

The Room, in common with Pinter's other single-act plays from this period, *The Dumb Waiter*, and *A Slight Ache*, consists of variations on the theme of an external threat. The characters desperately wish to maintain their regular routine, however boring it may be. They unsuccessfully attempt to resist the incipient or overt threat arising from newness or scepticism or a good dose of reality. The threat will inevitably penetrate the vulnerable surface of certainty the characters erect around themselves with language and repetitive actions. In 'Writing for the Theatre', a speech delivered at the Seventh National Student Drama Festival in Bristol on 4 March 1962, Pinter focuses upon his idea of verification and the uses of language. He says that he aims to create 'A language . . . where, under what is said, another thing is being said' (*VV*: 24).

Once violence takes place, words become meaningless. Rose and Bert, her husband in *The Room*, don't fully exhibit the full range of their selves till they confront and destroy the intruder, Riley the blind Negro. Pinter, in an interview, on the BBC on 19 August 1960, with Kenneth Tynan (1927–1980), at the time a highly influential critic, said that he is dealing 'with these characters at the extreme edge of their living' (cited Esslin, *Pinter: A Study of His Plays*, 1977: 34). Characters are forced to face reality without the normal props of everyday living they have erected. However, Pinter leaves the outcome to his audience's imagination. Rose and Bert in their room have constructed a barrier of words and routine around themselves. Her nervous inconsequential banter has created deafness in Bert, her husband. Their world is one of utter boredom. She says 'No, it's not bad. Nice weak tea. Lovely weak tea. Here you are. Drink it down. I'll wait for mine. Anyway, I'll have it a bit stronger.' Here pauses, silences, staccato sentences receive no response except silence. She rambles on often in repetitive monosyllables and pronouns, both of which are linguistic characteristics of Pinter's work. 'This is a good room. You've got a chance in a place like this . . . No, you've got a window there, you can move yourself, you can come home at night, if you have to go out, you can do your job, you can come home, you're all right. And I'm here. You stand a chance' (9, 11).

In *The Peopled Wound*, Martin Esslin identifies eight forms of repetition in Pinter. Repetition is used as a device to convey information; as a reflection of characters struggling to articulate their feelings; as a reflection of enjoyment with the sound or feel of a word; as a hysterical reaction; as an indication of understanding or comprehension; as a form of refrain demonstrating consideration of an idea or an assertion; as an indication of 'a lack of emotion' allowing 'a train of associations to evolve; and when a character is lying'. This device permeates Pinter's work as do pauses and silences.[3] Although Pinter has come to regard the perception of his pauses and silences as exaggerated, they play a key role in his work.

In *The Room*, a knock sounds on the door, and Rose is frightened. The name Rose itself has East End Jewish reverberations and the landlord's mother in the play might have also been Jewish. Pinter, however, keeps the threat universal, undefined and non-ethnic. The landlord Mr. Kidd enters the room: Bert has heard Kidd and Rose talk frequently and largely remains silent. Rose is even sceptical of what Kidd says: 'I don't believe he had a sister, ever.' Neither Rose nor the audience can verify or even deny Kidd's claims. Rose's uncertainty about the world outside the room is increased by the entrance of Mr. and Mrs. Sands:

Rose: What's it like out?

Mrs. Sands: It's very dark out.

Mr. Sands: No darker than in.

Truth becomes a matter of personal perception: Mrs. Sands, for instance, explains their arrival, an encounter with a man down in the basement. In the last sentence of her monologue, she claims that she and her husband were on their way down the stairs. Rose, however, remembers that Mrs. Sands earlier said that they were going up and not down, consequently placing her entire account in doubt (16, 19).

Pinter's work is open to a myriad of interpretations. One perception of *The Room* that it reflects his own guilt concerning the consequences of his marriage upon his parents and his own break with the Thistlewaite Road of his upbringing where he largely spent his first 25 years produced a counter response from Pinter. Pinter has 'always seen Riley', he comments, 'as a messenger, a potential saviour who is trying to release Rose from the imprisonment of the room and the restrictions of her life with Bert' her husband. Pinter adds that Riley is 'inviting her to come back to her spiritual home; which is why he gets beaten up when Bert returns. But, to me, Riley has always been a redemptive figure, and that was how I staged it when I later came to direct it with Vivien', to whom the published text is dedicated 'and a fine black actor called Thomas Baptiste' (cited *B*: 69).

There certainly is xenophobia in *The Room*. Rose is proud that 'we keep ourselves to ourselves' (21), and is afraid the basement may contain 'foreigners' (9). She tells Riley 'You're not only a nut . . . you're a blind nut and you can get out the way you came' (30). The remarkable thing is that Pinter conveys the fear humorously and yet fearfully with an underlying sadness. Rose's remark contains Pinter's humour found in his repetitive usage and the word 'nut', but is also disturbing. In the later *monologue* the man alone in his chair has an obsession with black girls dressed in leather who seem to ride on motorcycles. Davies in *The Caretaker* rails against foreigners whom he believes are taking over, although of course he may be one of them himself. Pinter's work is pervaded with fear and human conflict, the fight for survival and space, especially embodied in the fear of the outsider and the foreigner.

In *The Room* an intruder, Riley, 'a blind Negro' (28), rather than a blind Irishman which his name might imply, although of course he could be a blind black Irishman, enters carrying a cryptic message for Rose, apparently from her 'father': 'Come home, Sal' (30). It is unclear whether Rose recognises Riley or not, whether she is indeed 'Rose' or 'Sal' or neither. Bert has been driving, an activity common among Pinter's male characters, and one of the few things they all seem capable of undertaking. Aware of 'Rose's' fears, Bert savagely and inexplicably kills Riley. This serves no purpose: Rose loses her sight. Even within the apparent protection of one's own room, external forces intrude. Pinter's 'ending' is open ended and suggestive, *The Room* echoes in the audiences' and readers' minds.

During this period, 1957, Pinter and his wife Vivien, in spite of occasional rep. company work, were very poor. Probably in July 1957 Pinter stayed for the night at the Bristol flat of the actress Susan Engel (1935–). Around midnight, he was woken to say that a friend appeared with his literary agent. In his tribute to Jimmy Wax who died in 1983, Pinter wrote: 'I put on a dressing gown and went into the kitchen. In the kitchen was Jimmy Wax. He told me he'd heard about *The Room* and suggested that Susan and I read a scene from the play.' Pinter adds, 'The next week Jimmy wrote proposing that he be my agent. I agreed . . . .. We then spoke daily and met weekly for almost twenty-six years.' Wax was Pinter's 'backbone, through thick and thin.' Pinter movingly adds, 'I shall never forget his warmth, his kindness, his constancy. He was a rare man, a true friend.' Pinter concludes that 'His death is, for me, "a very limb lopp'd off"' (*Jimmy*: 49–50). Following Jimmy Wax's death, Pinter's agent became the ever protective Judy Daish, who had worked for Wax for 5 years before founding her own literary agency. In addition to publishing *Landscape* (1968), Wax was the dedicatee of *No Man's Land* (1975). Pinter dedicated the fictional *The Dwarfs* (1990) to Judy Daish.

Around this time, Pinter gained the support of the highly influential English dramatic critic Harold Hobson (1904–1992), who was the chief theatre critic for the *Sunday Times*. *The Room* was performed on 30 December 1957 at the National Student Drama Festival held that year at Bristol University. The *Sunday Times* sponsored the festival, attended by Hobson who wrote that *The Room* 'makes one stir uneasily in one's shoes, and doubt for a moment, the comforting solidity of the earth' (cited *B*: 74). Pinter was living with a very pregnant wife in a Notting Hill Gate basement flat. The review attracted the attention of the producer Michael Codron (1930–) who arranged to meet Pinter and Wax. Pinter sent him *The Party*, this became *The Birthday Party*. Pinter had also completed *The Dumb Waiter*. Following the birth of their son Daniel, on 29 January 1958, the Pinters moved to a first-floor flat in the Chiswick High Road. Codron agreed to put on *The Birthday Party*. Pinter commented, 'My life just changed' (cited Esslin: *Pinter: A Study of His Plays*, 1977: 17).

The Dumb Waiter

The single-act *The Dumb Waiter*, written just after the longer *The Birthday Party*, is more complex than *The Room*. Fear and threat dominate. Gus and Ben create their own brand of cut and thrust humour as a defence against the world although they are hired killers. As long as they can chatter away, then they need not think about their own situation. Ben says, 'I've got my woodwork. I've got my model boats. Have you ever seen me idle? I'm never idle. I know how to occupy my time, to its best advantage' (40). They are afraid of an unnamed boss. A mysterious voice at the other end of a speaking tube barks out commands. Gus and Ben communicate about events in a newspaper, or a football game. They reminisce about a once great

Aston Villa team conjuring up a past gone forever. The revelries are broken by the voice coming to them through a tube at the other end of the dumb waiter. Pinter develops cosmic reverberations from the most mundane situation, such as a demand for chops. They ask, 'Yes, but what happens when we're not here? What do they do then? All these menus coming down, and nothing going up. It might have been going on like this for years' (57). They prepare for the entrance of an intruder who is to be killed. Gus, however, becomes the intruder and the curtain comes down as the two fight a battle of life and death for dominance and survival.

A Slight Ache

Another short play *A Slight Ache* is based upon an un-produced radio-play entitled *Something in Common* and belongs to 1958. In this, violence is not overt. The uneducated Gus and Ben are replaced by the well-educated Edward and his wife Flora. Their class status doesn't protect them from a failure to communicate or to be able to control their life or fate. *A Slight Ache* contains passages of lyrical, poetic expression that re-emerge in *Landscape* and *Silence* and Pinter's subsequent work. The play opens with repetition:

> *Flora*   Have you noticed the honeysuckle this morning?
>
> *Edward*   The what?
>
> *Flora*   The honeysuckle.
>
> *Edward*   Honeysuckle? Where?
>
> *Flora*   By the back gate, Edward.
>
> *Edward*   Is that honeysuckle? I thought it was . . . convolvulus, or something.

These floral associations suggest traditional poetic pastoral allusions and motifs. In a truncated fashion, Pinter suggests a resonant yet possibly menacing lyrical expression, seen, for instance, in Flora's

'The whole garden's in flower this morning. The clematis. The convolvulus. Everything.' Such images are juxtaposed with the mundane: 'Pass the tea pot, please.' (9–10) Then there is a wasp in the marmalade: the wasp is the initial ominous intruder of the day. Both Edward and Flora respond with silence. With the wasp, a prefiguring device, comes Edward's 'slight ache' in the eyes (12). Here as in his other drama, Pinter uses sight imagery as a motif conveying impotence. Edward scalds the wasp with boiling water, kills it and finds relief. Flora, on the other hand, sees this action as an 'awful' experience (14).

Edward then becomes aware of the apparently harmless match seller, a constant presence in the road behind the house. Edward perceives the match seller as a threat. A further suggestive allusion lies in the apparent fact that the street in which the match seller stands leads to a monastery. Edward, an author with philosophical pretensions, is writing on space and time, tries to understand the match seller. For Flora, he appears as a 'bullock' (17), a representative of her own sexual yearning. Edward decides to introduce the man into his study to cross-examine him. Flora is increasingly attracted physically to the unknown man. Edward's interview with him focuses upon the matches he sells. Flora projects her desires on the match seller: 'It's me you are waiting for, wasn't it? You've been standing waiting for me.' Sexual insults, intimidation and foul language occur frequently in Pinter's work. Edward tells Flora, 'You lying slut. Get back to your trough!' (32–33).

Power continually shifts between Edward and the intruder. Edward's monologues become increasingly rambling, incoherent and weaker. He projects his own emotional state upon the man, the intruder whose back is turned to him. Edward returns to a period, for instance, when he claims to have felt nature and flowers, however he recounts that the dust enters his backgate 'and the long grass, scything together', as the death of his senses, overcame him (39). As Edward grows weaker, the match seller seems to grow stronger and actually rises from the bed where he has taken refuge. Edward is then given the match tray, the symbol of the outsider, the dispossessed, the impotent. The once-outside-the-room match seller then usurps Edward's position with his wife Flora. Edward's premonition has proved correct in a similar fashion to the premonitions and fears of Rose, Gus and Ben in *The Room*. The outsider is capable of destroying the world we have created ourselves and so tenaciously attempted to protect. *The Room*, *The Dumb Waiter* and *A Slight Ache* in common with most of Pinter's work remain open ended, capable of manifold interpretation. The match seller, for instance, can represent death as well as sexuality. Flora's monologues exhibit Pinter's poetic lyrical quality, more so than in *The Room* and *The Dumb Waiter*. Pinter is more than a recorder of various speech patterns of London English: he is a theatrical poet.

The Hothouse

Before turning to *The Birthday Party* that marks Pinter's recognition by a wider audience and is his first real masterpiece, attention should be drawn to *The Hothouse*. This began as a project, an hour-long BBC Radio Play submitted for consideration in November 1958. Set in a psychological research centre and featuring experiments and interrogation, it draws upon Pinter's own experiences in 1954 at the Maudsley Hospital in London where he went as a guinea pig in order to earn desperately needed money. Following the mauling, *The Birthday Party* received the hands of most of the London theatre critics, Pinter discarded the play. In 1980, he directed its premier at the Hampstead Theatre. In 1997, it was performed at the Chichester Festival Theatre with Pinter in the main role of Colonel Roote who is in charge of the sinister government run psychiatric hospital that is the setting for the play. It was revived at the National Theatre in July 2007 with Stephen Moore (1937–), as Roote and Finbar Lynch (1959–), playing the role of the smooth, potentially sensual deputy. The play is comic, veering towards farce in the mode of Monty Python. It anticipates by nearly 30 years Pinter's depiction of the abuses of the state in *Mountain Language* (1988). *The Hothouse* provides 'the missing link among Harold Pinter's plays'. Charles Spencer reviewing the National Theatre revival in the *Daily Telegraph* writes that 'What makes the piece so fascinating is that it seems to unite Pinter's early plays of largely unspecified, enigmatic menace with the later . . . political plays, in which he specifically depicts the cruelty of the state against the individual' (19 July 2007: www.dailytelegraph.com).

The Birthday Party

The first performance of *The Birthday Party* took place on 28 April 1958 at the Arts Theatre, Cambridge. Directed by Peter Wood (1927–), Meg was performed by Beatrix Lehmann (1903–1979), Stanley by Richard Pearson (1918–), and Goldberg by John Slater (1916–1975). The play then moved to Oxford where it was also well received, moving to the Lyric Theatre, Hammersmith on 19 May and closing after one week. The influential drama critic of the London *Evening Standard*, Milton Shulman (1913–2004), wrote in a review entitled 'Sorry, Mr. Pinter, You're Just Not Funny Enough', that, 'sitting through *The Birthday Party* at the Lyric Hammersmith, is like trying to solve a crossword puzzle where every vertical clue is designed to put you off the horizontal.' Shulman continues, 'It will be best enjoyed by those who believe that obscurity is its own reward. Others may not feel up to the mental effort needed to illuminate the coy corners of this opaque, sometimes macabre comedy' (20 May 1958: 6).

However, Harold Hobson reviewing *The Birthday Party* in the *Sunday Times* shortly after Shulman's negative comments defended the play. Hobson writes 'Mr. Pinter has got hold of a primary fact of existence. We live on the verge of disaster.' Hobson's observations titled 'The Screw Turns Again', penetrate with remarkable insight to the core of much of Pinter's work:

> There is something in your past – it does not matter what – which will catch up with you. Though you go to the uttermost parts of the earth, and hide yourself in the most obscure lodgings in the least popular of towns, one day there is a possibility that two men will appear. And someone will be looking for *them*, too. There is terror everywhere . . . . The fact that no one can say precisely what it is about, or give the address from which the intruding Goldberg and McCann come, or say precisely why it is that Stanley is so frightened by them is, of course, one of its greatest merits. It is exactly in this vagueness that its spine-chilling quality lies (25 May 1958: 11).

In a letter written to Peter Wood dated 30 March 1958 written just before rehearsal started for the first production of *The Birthday Party* in April 1958, Pinter makes valuable comments on the character of Stanley and the drama in general. Its author refuses to explain or to defend Stanley's reasons for attempting to escape into a depressing, obscure seaside boarding-house: 'Stanley *cannot* perceive his only valid justification – which is, he is what he is – therefore he certainly can never be articulate about it.' Pinter tells Wood that Stanley 'is not *articulate*. The play in fact merely states that two men come down to take away another man and do so.' However, 'The play dictated itself, but I confess that I wrote it – with intent, maliciously, purposefully, in command of its growth.' Pinter then adds:

> [Stanley] does possess, however, for my money, a certain fibre – he fights for his life. It doesn't last long, this fight. His core being a quagmire of delusion, his mind a tenuous fusebox, he collapses under the weight of their accusation – an accusation compounded of the shitstained strictures of centuries of 'tradition.' Though non-conformist, he is neither hero nor exemplar of revolt. Nothing salutary for the audience to identify itself with. And *yet*, at the same time, I believe that a greater degree of identification will take place than might seem likely. A great deal, it seems to me, will depend on the actor. If he copes with Stanley's loss of himself successfully, I believe a certain amount of poignancy will emanate. Couldn't we all find ourselves in Stanley's position at any given moment? (*VV*: 12–15)

There are specifics in the play. McCann is of Irish origins, Goldberg draws upon a East End Jewish identity. His memories are of Hackney with recollections of Uncle Barney who had a feeling for 'Shabbus' (29). Goldberg's partner makes anti-semitic remarks referring to 'Judas' (55). Goldberg refers to Basingstoke (29), a sleepy middle class town on a main route to the south coast. Yet his memories, his speech rhythms indicate that he is a product of Hackney, although he is attempting to assimilate into the wider world. In the opening act Goldberg's reminiscences contain explicit to the railings and canal (they echo subsequent passages in Pinter) and to the Hackney dog track. Goldberg's memories elevate to a moment of muted lyricism 'The sun falling behind the dog stadium. Ah!' (46).

From Goldberg's perspective, Stanley and Meg are transformed into Jews. Goldberg's East End intonation takes over. He tells them:

> We've heard a lady extend the sum total of her devotion, in all its pride, plume and peacock, to a member of her own living race. Stanley, my heartfelt congratulations. I wish you, on behalf of us all, a happy birthday. I'm sure you've never been a prouder man than you are today. Mazletov! And may we meet only at Simchahs! (*The Birthday Party*, 1960: 50).

Goldberg's rhythms and diction, 'her own living race', 'never been a prouder man', 'Mazletov!' and 'may we meet only at Simchahs!' provide a pointer to his identity. His speech is applauded by Meg and Lulu who probably don't understand terms such as 'Mazletov' (good luck) and 'Simchahs' (happy occasions) (59).

In Act *III* McCann refers to Goldberg as 'Simey' to which Goldberg violently reacts, 'NEVER CALL ME THAT!' (79). He is reacting to the snide play on the name Simon. Goldberg is attempting to shed his past, to escape from it, but the past continually reappears. He remembers his father's dying words to him: 'Never, never forget your family, for they are the rock, the constitution and the core!' (81). Goldberg's sons appear in the earlier but not in subsequent texts of *The Birthday Party*. They seem to have forgotten their father and their origins. His sons and his love for 'Emanuel' found, for instance, in the first paperback edition play of 1963 (30), don't appear in the second revised edition published 2 years later. In his *Paris Review* interview of 1966 with Lawrence M. Bensky, Pinter remarks that 'The only play which gets remotely near to a structural entity which satisfies me is *The Homecoming*. *The Birthday Party* and *The Caretaker* have too much writing . . .. I wish to iron it down, eliminate things' (21). The cuts in *The Birthday Party* appear to be more verbal than structural in order to universalise and make the past vaguer. The elimination of Goldberg's sons illustrates this.

Goldberg turns on Stanley for apparently betraying his wife, his mother, his origins: 'Webber! Why did you change your name?' and also his religious faith – assuming Stanley ever had one. Stanley's past is deliberately left vague, although his family name 'Webber!' (53) may well indicate Jewish origins. In Pinter's poem about *The*

Birthday Party entitled 'A View of the Party', dated 1958, the poet writes: 'For Stanley had no home. | Only where Goldberg was, | And his bloodhound McCann, | Did Stanley remember his name?' (*VV*: 149).

In spite of the vagueness of the play, its interweaving of specific ethnic memory with the universal, *The Birthday Party* represents Pinter's ability to tackle larger dramatic forms. Rather than two major characters, as in the shorter plays, there are six. Instead of a single act running for maybe 45 minutes, there are three acts running for around two hours or more. In spite of Pinter's dissatisfaction with the structure of *The Birthday Party*, it has an ABA pattern, for instance, found in music. The drama starts with a given situation, seemingly calm, but replete with signs of doom. It then explodes in a burst of action, and the play returns to the initial situation, now substantially modified. The first-act dialogue includes Stanley who doesn't comply with the routine of Petey and Meg and reshapes it in his own way.

From early on in this act, the audience knows that two new guests are expected. Gradually, this fact increases in importance as it comes to the surface of Stanley's irritated comments, concerning the poor breakfast that Meg offers him (17). Stanley's sudden mood transitions keep the audience guessing as to what is to happen next. There is coyness, forgetfulness, threats, nagging, coarseness, all suggested in a few lines of dialogue and gesture. Stanley's abruptness of tonal change is evident: 'Tell me, Mrs. Boles, when you address yourself to me, do you ever ask yourself who exactly you are talking to? Eh?' (22). Towards the conclusion of the first act, Goldberg and McCann, the unexpected guests, have appeared. Suspense is developed by their referring to the 'job' they have come to do (29). They become part of the décor of the room. The attention then shifts back to Stanley, not through what he says but what he does. His obsessive drum-beats denote a reaction to Goldberg and McCann and to the frustration that has been building up throughout the first act. The drum-beats form the groundwork for the violence of the middle act.

In the 'B' section, the second act, there is a nagging, a bullying as Stanley and his tormentors Goldberg and McCann jostle for position. A series of questions lead to a crescendo, an exchange of blows revealing that words do not culminate in the truth. Physical conflict, violence appear to be the only certainty or truth in Pinter's universe. Games playing, singing, physical movement, shouting and the theatrical yet frightening usage of McCann's torch (rather in the manner of a car's headlights upon a darkened stage) take place. The enigmatic 'Curtain' (68) at the end of the act leaves open the issue of what Goldberg and McCann may do to Stanley or to one another.

In the final act, the 'C' section, calm seems to have returned. There are however, profound transformations beneath an apparently calm surface. How Goldberg and McCann have produced the 'new' Stanley (86), have transformed him, remains mysterious. Apart from Goldberg's flare up with McCann (88), routine is the norm. Lulu's assertions have no real bite and Stanley seems to return to the oblivion from whence he apparently came: possibly only memories remain. Perceptions are false and misleading. Two days following the Lyric, Hammersmith opening of *The Birthday Party*, Pinter wrote to Donald McWhinnie (1920–1987), of the BBC, who subsequently produced *A Night Out* in March 1960: 'the play has come a cropper, as you know.' Even this is untrue in perspective, as *The Birthday Party* is still being produced (21 May 1958: cited Esslin: *Pinter: A Study of His Plays*: 18).

Chapter Four
Success

The Caretaker

The Caretaker brought Pinter success and security. It was written during 1959 and initially presented by the Arts Theatre Club in association with Michael Codron and David Hall at the Arts Theatre Club on 27 April 1960 directed by Donald McWhinnie. The Arts Theatre production was very favourably reviewed. John Rosselli writing, for instance, in the *Manchester Guardian* on 29 April 1960 that *The Caretaker* is 'a fine play . . . . Pinter's work literally fascinates' (13). *The Caretaker* transferred to the Duchess Theatre in the West End on 30 May 1960. It won the *Evening Standard* Drama Award for the Best Play 1960 and ran for 444 performances. Kenneth Tynan, who previously in *The Observer* (25 May 1958: 15), had written a very hostile review of *The Birthday Party*, wrote in *The Observer*, 5 June 1960, in a review entitled 'A Verbal Wizard in the Suburbs': 'With *The Caretaker* . . . Harold Pinter has begun to fulfil the promise that I signally failed to see in *The Birthday Party* 2 years ago.' Tynan adds, 'In *The Caretaker*, symptoms of paranoia are still detectable . . . but their intensity is considerably abated; and the symbols have mostly retired to the background. What remains is a play about people' (16).

The Caretaker has been performed more often than any other Pinter play. Its genesis lies in Pinter's life when writing it in 1959. He was living with Vivien and their young son at 373 Chiswick High Road, in a first-floor flat. Pinter recalls: 'There was a chap who owned the house: a builder, in fact, like Mick who had his own van and whom I hardly ever saw. The only image I had of him was of this swift mover up and down the stairs and of his van going . . . Vrooom

. . . as he arrived and departed.' Pinter then adds, 'His brother lived in the house. He was a handyman . . . he managed rather more successfully than Aston, but he was very introverted, very secretive, had been in a mental home some years before and had had some kind of electrical shock treatment.' This brother 'did bring a tramp back one night. I call him a tramp, but he was just a homeless old man who' remained in the house for nearly a month. Pinter met him from time to time 'on the stairs . . . that was the only place you could ever meet.' The old man 'wasn't anywhere near as eloquent as Davies' however, in what must appear to be a very Pinteresque understatement, he adds: 'he didn't seem very content with his lot.' What remained with Pinter was the image 'of the open door to this room with the two men standing in different parts of the room doing different things . . . the tramp rooting in a bag and the other men looking out of the window and simply not speaking . . . A kind of moment frozen in time that left a very strong impression.'

Clearly, Pinter is not unsympathetic to the originals for Aston and Davies. Mick is almost pure invention. Pinter felt a sort of kinship with the old man whom theatrically he transforms into Davies. Subsequently, Pinter 'met him one day on Chiswick roundabout' after he'd been chucked out of 373 Chiswick High Road. After asking him 'how he was getting on', Pinter recalls that he didn't mention the drama 'because he wouldn't have known what a play was.' Pinter 'was writing on my old typewriter – with Daniel crawling about under my feet – and the round of the Labour Exchange and the odd half-pint at the Robin Hood and Little John [pubs] down the road. It was a very threadbare existence . . . very . . . . I was totally out of work. So I was very close to this old derelict's world, in a way.'

Pinter's empathy towards the original of Aston is revealed in the information that Aston whose real name was Austin, after he discovered that Pinter was a 'script writer' installed a telephone in the house. 'He'd only done it because he also knew I was in the business of writing; and he was very proud of that.' Vivien however felt that Pinter had betrayed Aston by using him in the play. According to Guy Vaesen, Vivien 'always detested *The Caretaker*'. In spite of the fact that it gave Pinter financial security, the success of the play displayed her own vulnerability. A power shift had occurred in Pinter's real life rather than in one of his dramas. He now was successful and

Vivien, the star of the rep. theatre, depended upon him, she was the lesser light. She also objected to her husband's use of personal experience as the foundation of his work. He also drew upon their marital conflict and transformed this creatively.

The fine actor Donald Pleasance (1919–1995): the original Davies who commented 'I loved playing Davies . . . because I've always been very interested in tramps', confirms Pinter's artistic rewriting of actual experience. Pleasance recalls that he 'used to drive Harold home after rehearsals.' One evening 'I suddenly remembered something: that I had been there before. I'd had my photograph taken there by an Indian photographer who had a very beautiful wife.' Pleasance continues, 'I suddenly realised these were the very same "blacks" whom Davies rails against and who were living on the other side of the wall to the real-life original' (cited *B*: 114–116, 127, 116). Such recollections also serve to reinforce the insight of Pinter's school rival Barry Supple who commented that a Pinter play is a 'great echo chamber' with its sources lying in 'the prosaic data of the dramatist's life history' (*Jewish Chronicle*, 25 June 1965: 31).

In *The Caretaker*, as in his other drama, Pinter achieves universality through the particular and the personal. Pinter remains true to the rhythms of thought and speech of his own background. For the 1962/1963 film version, Pinter chose his old neighbourhood, Hackney, rather than Chiswick as the setting. In the play, there are continual references to Hackney coming from the mouth of Mick. Davies, the tramp, the *schnorrer* (beggar) is a continual wanderer, continually on the move, forever condemned to search for something. Aston's room is just one more depressing room he has briefly occupied prior to eviction. The more he wants to find what he thinks he is searching for, the more elusive it becomes.

Davies is skilled at the act of survival. His explanation of this art produces humour. He tells Aston that 'The only way to keep a pair of shoes on, if you haven't got no laces, is to tighten the foot, see? Walk about with a tight foot, see? Well', he explains 'that's no good for the foot. Puts a bad strain on the foot. If you can do the shoes up proper, there's less chance of you getting a strain' (68). There is a repetitious, obsessive quality in Davies's speech: his questions are more of the nature of assertions. He is unable to explain his past, his present or his future to the people he meets, whom he is dependent on.

Davies wanders all over London and its surroundings in the quest for subsistence. Formal institutions, represented by the monastery at Luton that didn't give him a fresh pair of shoes, or the job market exemplified by a series of low paying jobs and petty fights relating to ownership, are not for him. Davies forlornly attempts to assert his dignity: 'Look here, I said to him, I got my rights: I told him that. I might have been on the road, but nobody's got more rights than I have.' His sense of his 'rights', his standing up to a perceived bully, is placed in the past. Words seem to be the only way in which he can assert himself. He is continually attempting to convince society that he is a person, that he exists. 'It's not my job to take out the bucket! . . .. My job's cleaning the floor, clearing up the tables, doing a bit of washing-up, nothing to do with taking out buckets!' There is a hierarchy that should be respected: 'Even if I was supposed to take out the bucket, who was this git to come up and give me orders? We got the same standing. He's not my boss! He's nothing superior to me' (9–10).

Davies's speeches are replete with the poetry of the particular which adds a moving dimension to the reality of his situation. He tells Aston, 'I took a short cut to Watford and picked up a pair [of shoes] there. Got onto the North Circular, just past Hendon, the sole come off, right where I was walking. Lucky I had my old ones wrapped up, still carrying them, otherwise I'd have been finished, man' (15). The specific locations, to places and specific roads north of London, and in North London itself, ground his plight in the real.

Davies is sensitive to questions about his past. Aston in an intimidating manner asks him, 'Welsh, are you?' Davies replies, 'Eh?' And Aston even shortens his question, making it more threatening, 'You Welsh?' To this Davies replies, 'Well, I have been around, you know . . . what I mean . . . I been about' (27). What Davies wants is to belong to the society that rejects him. Consequently, Davies demonstrates a negative reaction to a question reflecting the need to place people, questions frequently asked by the police. Instinctively, Davies asserts his own individuality.

Somewhat ironically, and perhaps predictably given his own insecurities, Davies exhibits racism. He refers to 'them Blacks' and 'aliens' (8). There is consequently a layer of society that he can look down upon, one even beneath him. Mick calls Davies a 'foreigner', a remark that provokes Davies to assert his Britishness (35). It is Mick who cruelly strips Davies of any illusions he may have had. He tells Davies 'You're a bloody impostor, mate!' He adds, 'I can take nothing you say at face value. Every word you speak is open to any number of different interpretations.' These words apply to Pinter's work generally. Mick continues to undercut Davies, to bring him down to size, and in doing so comments, albeit unwittingly upon himself and many other Pinter characters: 'Most of what you say is lies. You're violent, you're erratic, you're just completely unpredictable. You're nothing else but a wild animal, when you come down to it' (76–77).

Of course, *The Caretaker*, in common with Pinter's other work, is about power and a power struggle for supremacy and control among the characters. As Stanley in *The Birthday Party*, the victim Davies quickly becomes the exploiter when the opportunity arises. The battle for control doesn't cease. Those at the bottom of the heap strive to change their situation and those at the top attempt to maintain their position. Davies utilises all his experience to play Mick and Aston off against each other. He even exploit's Aston's mercy when he feels it necessary and feasible to do so. In short, Davies bites the hand that feeds him.

Davies's language, as that of Mick and Aston, is permeated with slang expressions, repetitions, grammatical errors, non sequiturs, pauses and silences. In a letter to the *Sunday Times*, 14 August 1960, Pinter writes, 'As far as I'm concerned, *The Caretaker* is funny up to a point. Beyond that point it ceases to be funny, and it was because of that point that I wrote it' (21). So underneath the humour lies the elemental struggle for power and survival expressed in Pinter's use of language, character and dramatic manipulation. Pinter told Bensky 'I agree that more often than not, the speech only *seems* to be *funny* – the man in question is actually fighting a battle for his life' (34).

The Caretaker is also a play about many other things other than the fight for survival. For instance, it expresses dreams and the necessity for fantasy. As with *The Birthday Party*, characters retreat into their private vision of the past or the present, shutting out others. For Pinter, the play deals with the caretaker and two brothers. Critics on the other hand provide an enormous variety of interpretation.

James T. Boulton writing in *Modern Drama* in 1963, in one of the earliest serious academic articles to be published on Pinter as opposed to daily or weekly reviews, accords Pinter the stature of a serious, important writer. For Boulton, Davies becomes an archetypal symbol of life's journey. Katherine H. Burkman in her *The Dramatic World of Harold Pinter* (1971), argues that the drama becomes a 'ritual battle for possession of place' (87). For Michael Billington, it is 'also a play that deals with one of the great themes of modern drama . . . the attempt to shield ourselves against diurnal reality through protective illusions' (122).

The more *The Caretaker* is performed, the more it is read in common with other great drama, the more varied are the interpretations and the more lines from the play reverberate in the memory in the way lines from Shakespeare do. The lines may refer to Sidcup, Davies's Jerusalem, or Mecca or to Mick's lyrical paeans of praise to London bus routes. 'She could get a 38, 581, 30 or 38A, take her down to the Essex Road to Dalston Junction in next to no time' (34). A mundane object such as a bucket, speculation on its being empty or not, the act of smashing an icon, a Buddha, take on a tremendous reverberating power of their own as does the natural human hope for a change in the weather.

The Caretaker transformed its writer's life. He now had public recognition and relative wealth. He had time to write. In the summer of 1960, he, Vivien and Daniel moved from the Chiswick High Road to a larger flat at Fairmead Court Kew adjacent to Kew Gardens. Three years later Pinter and his family moved again, this time to a Regency house on the Sussex coast, 14 Ambrose Place, Worthing, just over a 5-minute walk from the sea shore. Pinter's next full-length play didn't appear until 1965. The beginning of Pinter's international recognition is best marked by the opening at Broadway's Lyceum Theatre on 4 October 1962 of *The Caretaker*. It ran for 5 months to excellent reviews. The same year, 1962, sees in December, the beginning of shooting, in Hackney, for the film *The Caretaker* (released in the United States in 1964 under the title *The Guest*) directed by Clive Donner (1926–). During the year, Pinter was also working on the screenplay of *The Servant*. He also wrote for television *The Lover*.

The Servant

Pinter's 1962 adaptation of Robin Maugham's *The Servant*, screened in 1963, represents Pinter's first adaptation of someone else's work. Subsequently, he is to adapt at least 16 other works for the screen. In an interview with Peter Florence in February 2004, Pinter reflects that he 'enjoyed the craft of transportation', of adaptation from one media, in this instance a novella, to a film script. In adaptation, he kept as far as possible with the spirit or essence of the original while being aware that the film media reveals the truth of a work by other means and from other perspectives. So good was his initial attempt that his first scripted film *The Servant* in 1964 gained in addition to the British Screenwriters Guild Award, the New York Film Critics' Best Writing Award.

In 1961 the director Michael Anderson (1920–), who had acquired the film rights of Maugham's work, commissioned a script from Pinter. Anderson was unable to obtain sufficient financial backing for the project and Joseph Losey (1909–1984), a refugee from the Hollywood anti-communist witch trials, who was blacklisted and domiciled in England, and subsequently to work on other films with Pinter, obtained the rights. Although they initially got off to a very shaky start, Losey thinking the screenplay Pinter had written for Anderson 'was seventy-five percent bad', they had a very fruitful, productive relationship. In his '*The Servant*: Notes on the Film', Losey singles out for praise Pinter's understanding of 'the usefulness of the overheard line: of dialogue used as sound effect' (cited Gale, *Films*, 2001: 30, 13). Both Pinter and Losey felt deeply about social injustice. Mutually too they brilliantly evoke the sense of place, possessions and rooms upon people. The film adaptation of *The Servant* also develops a preoccupation found in *The Collection* (1961). The adaptation focuses on the politics of domestic relationships and the ambiguity of sexuality.

Further, as in his plays, Pinter utilises in his adaptation of *The Servant*, what is referred to in a *Transatlantic Review* interview on 'Filming *The Caretaker*' (13 [Summer 1963]), as the 'silent music' (20) of pauses and implied meanings, as well as the music of snatches of absurd interspersed conversation and the counterpoint of recordings – then played on the now outdated gramophone. The lines of the song

'Leave it alone | It's all gone . . . Can't love without you | Must love without you' pervade the total film accentuating the meaning of the action at important moments. A similar technique is used, for instance, in Pinter's later play *Old Times* (1970–1971) which is permeated with Gershwin and Kern songs.

The Collection

Much of Pinter's subsequent preoccupations are found in his earlier plays and film adaptations. Take, for instance, *The Collection* first presented by Associated Rediffusion Television on 11 May 1961 with Vivien Merchant in the role of Stella desired by the male characters and who probably has an affair with at least one of them, Bill. There are power games played out, plus sexual ambiguities in the drama. Bill may well be a homosexual who is prepared to be perceived as the lover of another man's wife. This gives him power over Harry whom he desires. An apparent affair creates jealousy in Stella's husband James who enters into a relationship with Bill which erupts in violence. The sexual personal ambiguities are set in the milieu of the East End garment district.

Pinter converted the television drama into one for the West End stage where it opened at the Aldwych Theatre directed for the Royal Shakespeare Company jointly by Pinter and Peter Hall on 18 June 1962. This marked the start of a very fruitful relationship between Pinter, the company and Hall who subsequently went on to direct *The Homecoming*, *Old Times*, *A Kind of Alaska*, *Family Voices*, *Victoria Station* among other work of Pinter.

The Lover

While working on the screenplay of *The Servant*, Pinter wrote *The Lover* for television. Broadcast on Associated Rediffusion Television on 28 March 1963 it won the coveted Prix Italia for television drama and several Guild of British Television Producers and Directors awards. It too focuses on the destructive consequences of routine and boredom. In this instance, Richard the husband gains his wife's assent to transform their humdrum life. He casts himself as the lover and Sarah his wife played, by Vivien Merchant, his private whore, thus satisfying their mutual wish for something new. Sarah consequently apparently finds fulfilment of her sexual fantasies without resorting to prostitution or taking on another lover. So she becomes whore and wife. At the conclusion of the play, the roles become confused.

The Pumpkin Eater

This obsession with fantasy and renewal, with sexual transference and ambiguity occurs too in *The Homecoming*. This was written just before and following Pinter, Vivien and the young Daniel's move to Worthing in 1963. At the same time, Pinter wrote the screenplay for *The Pumpkin Eater*, a novel by Penelope Mortimer (1928–1999), published in 1962. Technically the novel presents Pinter with a special challenge. Its subject, the need to make babies, demands a special feminine empathy. It is a first-person narrative that Pinter confessed during his interview with Peter Florence as having little sympathy with. There is a first-person voice-over. Pinter as the adapter attempts to give an objective account of what takes place in the novel, the first-person narrative is transformed into the verbal conflict going on between the characters. It was, Pinter says in his introduction to his *Collected Screenplays*, 'shot exactly as written' with shots of the house leading up to the bedroom (24). His script attempts to convey the visceral agitation, the pain and impossibility of achieving a solution to that which is happening in the house. The film highlights the novel's depiction of adultery and betrayal. The innumerable pauses and silences are Pinter's, not Penelope Mortimer's.

The Homecoming

Penelope Mortimer told a reporter from the *Daily Telegraph* that '*The Pumpkin Eater* is about the progression of the married state' (3 September 1971: 11). Pinter somewhat ironically, given his preoccupations at the time, responded to a journalist's question concerning his reasons for undertaking the script in the first place. He comments: 'because it's about marriage. And marriage is important. I mean a lot of people do it' (*Daily Mail*, 7 March 1964: 8). *The Homecoming* too focuses on sexual ambiguity, nuances and betrayal. The play for Pinter has very close associations with Worthing, with Joseph Brearley and Pinter's own marriage. Pinter recalls 'sitting in my big room in Worthing.' His old school teacher came to visit him 'and read *The Homecoming* and I was at the other end of the room reading something else. I had only one copy of the play. I'll never forget he finished it, slammed it down and walked out of the front door.' Pinter didn't see him for another three quarters of an hour. 'But he'd been so affected by the play that he had to get a blow of sea air' (cited *B*: [155]–156).

The Homecoming opened at the Aldwych Theatre, London, directed by Peter Hall on 3 June 1965. It followed a pre-London run in Cardiff on 25 March 1965 and subsequently was transferred to Broadway where it opened on 3 January 1966 winning three major awards. In common with *The Caretaker*, it takes place in North London: in this instance, in the living-room of 'an old house'. The time is the late summer, the cricket season has wound down, the football season has just started up, the horse racing season gives way to urban evenings at the dog track. In such an atmosphere, violence is latent but immediately in the drama comes to the surface. Lenny, 'a man in his early thirties' tells the much older Max, 'a man of seventy' – 'Why don't you shut up, you daft prat?' This is both humorous and nasty. The reply is threatening and the threat is aided by a stage prop, Max's 'stick' which he 'lifts' and 'points' at Lenny while saying 'Don't you talk to me like that. I'm warning you.' The repetition of the pronoun adds force to the implicit threat but hasn't the humour and vitriolic quality of the London slang word 'prat' ([6] –7). The language of threat, intimidation and insult derives from the East End of London of the pre- and post-Second World War period. It reflects in its way the political situation of the Fascist–Communist confrontations of the thirties and forties and the career of the notorious and violent criminals the Kray Brothers who committed vicious crimes while operating a mafia type gang in the London of the 1950s and 1960s.

Max's memory is concerned with racing rather than cricket. He reflects, 'I used to live on the course. One of the loves of my life' implying of course that there were others, which he certainly is not going to reveal too much about to his sons! 'Epsom? I knew it like the back of my hand. I was one of the best-known faces down at the paddock. What a marvellous, open-air life.' The great race course associated with royalty provides an escape from the city. Max can indulge in his fantasies of the excitement of gambling and rubbing shoulders with those in power, the upper classes and aristocracy, the nouveau riche, thugs and all of those who take pleasure in horse racing (9).

Such desire to be in contact with those higher on the social ladder, to smoke the best cigars, a pleasure of both Max and Sam, 'a man of sixty-three' ([6]), to be the 'best chauffeur' rather than 'driver' (13), is combined with latent violence. The desire reflects fundamental feelings of personal and social unhappiness reflected on the universal and specific level in the drama. In this way, Pinter is reflecting his own background. As his school contemporary Barry Supple wrote in his outline of the plot of *The Homecoming*, 'Teddy, now a professor of philosophy in America, returns home to his cockney family after 6 years, bringing his (English) wife, whom no one in his family has yet met, because the marriage took place secretly on the eve of his departure' (*Jewish Chronicle*, 25 June 1965: 7).

Max seems not to notice that his son is married and accuses Teddy of bringing 'dirty tarts' into his house (42). Subsequently in the play, Max tells his son 'Listen, you think I don't know why you didn't tell me you were married? I know why.' Max's explanation is couched in general terms: 'You were ashamed. You thought I'd be annoyed because you married a woman beneath you. You should have known me better. I'm broadminded. I'm a broadminded man' (59). Barry Supple provides an explanation that Max fails to provide: 'The family is Jewish', but Ruth, Teddy's wife, is not (7, 31).

Pinter prefers to universalise the meaning of *The Homecoming* rather than to be too specific, partly as he doesn't wish to offend the sensibility of his friends to whom he is very loyal and partly because he does not wish to limit the universality of the play to a restrictive ethnic framework. Pinter does admit that the image of Max, a chauffeur, may well have been based on Moishe (Morris) Wernick's father, a London taxi driver. In fact, Morris Wernick, Pinter's friend from childhood days, wrote many years later, 'I married in 1956 and left immediately to start life in Canada. I never told my father that I was married [to a non-Jew] and for the' following decade, 'continued to keep up this "pretence" even on my infrequent visits to England.' In 1964, he brought his wife and children to meet his father for the first time. Reflecting in the early years of the twenty-first century, Wernick who spent his career as a university professor of English in Canada, observes 'Forty years ago marrying "out" was still not regarded lightly' (cited *B*: 163–164). Tremendous psychological pressures were placed upon sons by parents and especially mothers to marry the 'right' girl.

The names used by Pinter in the play rather give the game away. 'Sam', 'Joey' and 'Jessie' have biblical derivations. 'Ruth', 'a woman in her early thirties' ([6]) whom Teddy brings home is the name of King David's non-Jewish Moabite mistress. For Barry Supple, *The Homecoming* 'drawing more explicitly than Pinter's other plays on the social and cultural problems of his generation, is essentially a play about intermarriage…the interaction between the family and the Gentile intruder, the basic clash of social facts and sexual tensions, create a framework within which the play's otherwise nightmarish ending assumes at least the semblance of meaning'. As 'the tensions of intermarriage produce the tensions, the plot and the resolutions of' *The Homecoming* (7), its structure forms a pattern of hostility, acceptance and fulfilment.

The first act focuses on hostility to Ruth. Max tells Teddy 'We've had a smelly scrubber in my house all night. We've had a stinking pox-ridden slut in my house all night.' Such venom represents a real threatening replacement of Max's dead wife. A reconciliatory 'cuddle' with Teddy closes the act on a seemingly amicable note (42–44). The second act focuses upon the acceptance of Ruth by the family and recognition of her potential. The outsider is absorbed into the family. A stage direction at the opening of the act and its first words indicate rapprochement: 'Max smiles at' Ruth and she tells Max 'that was a very good lunch'. Max replies, 'I'm glad you liked it' ([45]–46). However, underneath such awkward civilities, the past continually smoulders in the shape of the family's memory of Jessica, Max's dead wife whom Ruth is gradually beginning to replace. This motif of a surrogate mother figure appears also in *The Birthday Party* and the radio-play *A Night Out* written in 1959 and broadcast in February 1960.

Ruth has created enormous resentment because she challenges fabrications of the past. Max at times reveals that the past was not so idyllic. For instance, he interrupts an argument between Ruth and Teddy concerning how marriage has changed them by saying 'Listen, live in the present, what are you worrying about? . . .. Who can afford to live in the past?' (50). These are ironic words because that is exactly what Max himself does for most of the time. Simultaneously, he demonstrates that he hasn't the strength to face up to the truth himself, and collapses in recognition of Sam's confirmation that 'MacGregor had Jessie in the back of my cab as I drove them along' (79). In a way, the family is opposed to Ruth for what she represents rather than for the vices which she shares with all of them, including Max's deceased wife. Family recognition comes about in direct proportion to the extent that each family member is prepared to renounce their illusory dreams and accept themselves as sinful or as human as anyone else.

After Ruth has achieved acceptance, she becomes part of the family fight for power, for who will be on top of the pecking order. Teddy, once the pride of the family, will be the first loser. Max boasts 'how many other houses in the district have got a Doctor of Philosophy sitting down drinking a cup of coffee?' (49). However, at the end of the play, Teddy finds himself cut out of the family circle which Ruth has taken over. Sex and money enable her to take control. The pattern of the play becomes the victory of the previously excluded and the expulsion of the insider, the eldest son, coupled with the destruction of the old power centre – Max the father. He, a crippled old man lying on the floor, pleads for Ruth's kiss. In the words of Barry Supple, 'Called a whore at the beginning, Ruth is established as one at the end; spurned as a slut when they first meet, she becomes the object of Joey's and Max's lust and promiscuity by the end' (7). She in fact seems to take on this role willingly, requesting 'a dressing-room, a rest-room, and a bedroom' adding 'all aspects of the agreement and conditions of employment would have to be clarified to our mutual satisfaction before we finalised the contract' (78). Indeed, Max realises that she is truly part of the family and their underlying attitudes when he tells her that she is 'not only lovely and beautiful, but you're kin. You're kith. You belong here' (76).

The Homecoming then presents a variation on the theme of the outsider at first rejected by society, who then achieves acceptance to the point of controlling and manipulating that society. The intellectual remains the outsider even where he grew up. The many symbolic and universal implications of the play are grounded in realistic speech patterns, in questions which are frequently rhetorical. Characters demand verification of what they said, as if they are unsure of the validity and veracity of their own assertions. Simple words are frequently repeated, often as questions and there are monologues extending for more than a few sentences, often pointing to incoherent and unreliable dreams of the past. An example of this repetitive rhythm of questioning may be found at the very beginning of the play. Max says: 'What have you done with the scissors?' This is followed by a 'Pause' and then 'I said I'm looking for the scissors. What have you done with them?' There is another 'Pause' followed by 'Did you hear me? I want to cut something out of the paper.' His son replies with, 'I'm reading the paper.' In other words, there are 37 words, 3 questions, 3 pauses opening the play, presenting the mundane but funny and vicious conflict between father and son. The duosyllabic words 'scissors' and 'something' achieve a special resonance. The former can cut, destroy and even kill; the 'something' ([7]) raises questions about what this play is going to be about.

Of course, there are many other examples running throughout the play. Lenny, for example, asks his father, 'That night . . . you know . . . the night you got me . . . that night with Mum, what was it like? Eh? When I was just a glint in your eye. What was it like? What was the background to it?' (36). The laughter comes probably out of a sense of embarrassment and shock as these are questions that many of us have never had the courage to ask. They reflect the way in which a Pinter play removes the veneer, the taboos of social and family existence, and manages to ask fundamental questions. Max's reply is shocking in its own way: 'You'll drown in your own blood' (37). This is both vicious and brutal. Interestingly, there is manuscript evidence revealing that Pinter repressed much more than actually appears in the script. At this point, he first typed 'stuff your face into glass' and then 'stuff your face with broken glass'. This was subsequently changed to 'shove it into a blade of glass' and then 'drown in your own bastard blood'.[4] The viciousness here and the violence is even more overt than in the final dramatic text, with the characters going for the jugular or the psychological weak points that they can detect in one another.

In the play, speeches of more than four lines tend to become transformed into idyllic dreams. Even Ruth enters into this mode, musing about her past activities as a model: 'This place . . . this house . . . was very big . . . the trees . . . there was a lake, you see . . . we used to change and walk down towards the lake . . . we went down a path.' She reflects: 'Oh, just . . . wait . . . yes . . .when we changed in the house, we had a drink. There was a cold buffet' (57). She too yearns for a world in which she is treated with dignity. Such lyrical dreams primarily focus on the pastoral and on the sexual. They alternate with short intense bouts of verbal conflict.

Naturally, there have been many interpretations of the play, some of which are focused on archetypal dreams and of the dramas obvious oedipal aspects. Others focus on, for instance, aspects of power play, family systems, feminist and gender-orientated concerns, to mention a few. In terms of Pinter's total *oeuvre*, *The Homecoming* has been in Peter Hall's words, regarded as Pinter's 'greatest and biggest play' (cited Batty: 165). Laden with memories of Hackney, Pinter brilliantly recreates these memories theatrically and transforms them into an enactment of dysfunctional family relationships. *The Homecoming* is his attempt to shred the Hackney past, to remove it from his system through depicting its most powerful entrapping institution, the family.

Chapter Five
Turning Points

The Homecoming represents something of a turning point in Pinter's work. His writing for a considerable period now focuses increasingly upon his private worlds rather than social ones. The retreat, as it were, into the mind coincides with an increasingly difficult time in his private life. In 1964, he moved with his family from Worthing to a large house in Hanover Terrace, Regent's Park. Antonia Fraser (1932–), who subsequently became Pinter's second wife, remembers 'It was the grandest house I've ever been in.' It must have been an extremely large house as Antonia Fraser being a member of the aristocracy had been to many. She adds, 'I went there once and it was absolutely, totally silent. I don't think I'd have understood *No Man's Land* if I hadn't seen it. Every room was immaculate with this terrible silence' (cited *B*: 180).

The Quiller Memorandum

Not only were there difficulties in Pinter's married life, but there were problems with his son who was becoming more and more anti-social and reclusive. Pinter in some ways retreated into work. He wrote the film script for Trevor Dudley-Smith's (1920–1995) 'Elleston Trevor', novel written under the pseudonym of 'Adam Hall' entitled *The Berlin Memorandum* published in 1965. This was transformed by Pinter into *The Quiller Memorandum* (1966) which essentially is an espionage film. It is the tale of an agent sent to Berlin to blow the cover of a neo-Nazi movement. Again, Pinter's preoccupations emerge in his film script: resistance to authority; suspense; power play and the strength of women; plus moral ambiguity.

In its concern with guilt, revenge and the past set in Germany, the play anticipates Pinter's subsequent 1987–1988 adaptation of Fred Uhlman's novel *Reunion*.

Accident

Similar general features may be also seen in Pinter's adaptation of Nicholas Mosley's (1923–) *Accident*. Pinter worked on the screenplay of *Accident* from 1965–1966 with Joseph Losey. *Accident* focuses on betrayals and varying accounts of what may or may not have occurred. The film opens with a car skidding and crashing near the home of an Oxford philosopher, Stephen Jervis. There were two people in the car who seem to have been on their way to visit Stephen. William, a student from an aristocratic background, is dead. The other, Anna, from an Austrian background, is rescued from the crash scene by Stephen. He takes her home, calms her and doesn't tell the police that she was at the crash scene.

There follows a flashback revealing that the three main characters have all been in some way or other involved with Anna. William, shortly before the crash, had become engaged to her. Stephen, her Oxford tutor, now married with two children, had unsuccessfully loved Anna. Charley, a fellow Oxford don, formerly Stephen's best friend, had a secret affair with Anna. As the film closes, it moves forward in time to the present. Following the accident, Stephen makes love to Anna while she is in a state of shock. He then manages to get her back into her college without being seen. This was the period in which female students would have been rusticated or sent down from Oxford if they had been caught away at night. The following morning, he and Charley, who is unaware of the crash and subsequent events, visit her. They discover that Anna is leaving Oxford. *Accident* closes with Stephen driving back, playing the role of a dutiful father. At the same time, the soundtrack conveys the car crash that will plague him with guilt for the rest of his life.

Pinter made some radial changes from Mosley's novel. First, he omits the first-person narrative used throughout by Mosley. Second, Pinter introduces Stephen's sexual assault on the traumatised Anna following the car crash. The assault takes place while Stephen's wife is in hospital giving birth. Third, Pinter omits Charley from the possibilities of perjury charges arising from Stephen's sense of guilt. Fourth, he stresses more than the first-person narrative time shifts between the present and the past. There is a cyclical structure moving from the crash and its aftermath to the past and then back to the consequences. Such differences emphasise Pinter's obsession with the craft of writing: with the art of adaptation from one media, the novel, to another, the film. They reveal his concern with sexual power and jealousy, the oppressor–victim motif, memories, adultery and guilt. Pinter doesn't apportion blame, but is depicting what has happened. He is determined not to 'stand as a judge'. Pinter wrote to Nicholas Mosley 'I have, I think seen it', and the events 'as something that happens, that has happened, something that has taken place'. Pinter adds, 'If I do not feel the end as optimistic, neither do I feel it as pessimistic. Something had taken place, something that will always live, on all levels' (cited *B*: 187).

It would be unfair to reduce Pinter's adaptation to bare essentials. The dialogue is crisp, staccato and played out against idyllic scenes of water, superb lawns, cricket squares (the Parks at Oxford) and other Oxford scenes such as the shadow of the Magdalen College Tower. Betrayals abound as when, for instance, Stephen returns from a sexual escapade in London to find Charley with Anna. Stephen, too, is haunted by his sense of age creeping up on him. There are scenes that practically omit words altogether. One that is particularly memorable occurs on a punt on the Isis and brilliantly depicts sexual tension between people, and desire played out with the river and river bank as a beautiful scenario.

In financial terms, the film failed, although it was awarded at Cannes the Grande Prix Spécial du Jury for 1967. There were mixed reviews, too. Wheeler Winston Dickson writing at the end of the twentieth century in his 'The Eternal Summer of Joseph Losey and Harold Pinter's *Accident*', finds the adaptation dated. He writes, 'The sexual ethics of the 1960s are everywhere apparent . . . blatant infidelity is routinely condoned, no one seems to use any sort of contraceptives, and the issue of sexually transmitted diseases is never broached' (Gale: *Films*: 35). Pinter received a total sum of £20,000, the author Nicholas Mosley only £2,700 for the rights. Previously, Robin Maugham received £11,500 for *The Servant* and Pinter a mere

£3,000. Now Pinter was in demand for his work in films and television. His work from the middle of the 1960s reveals the greater impact of the visual media. Another sign of recognition was that in June 1966 Pinter was created a Commander of the Order of the British Empire (CBE). At the turn of the century, he was to reject with disdain such official establishment blandishments, for instance a knighthood, offered by the then Prime Minister, Tony Blair.

The Basement

During 1966, Pinter wrote *The Basement* for BBC-2 TV. Again, there are the usual Pinter preoccupations: three participants in a sexual triangle; power and dominance; the fight between two men for space and seeming control of a woman. There is also an increasing terseness and economy of means with each word, action and movement appearing to take on its own significant reverberation and implication. In *The Basement* Law, the central figure, becomes a victim of what he has been afraid of in the first place, the domination by another person possessing a stronger personality, and he has to learn to face up to and to deal somehow with this experience. *The Basement* and *Accident* point to a new direction too in Pinter's work. The characters are no longer East Enders rooted in the East End but very wealthy, inhabiting the world of Oxford or elsewhere. They are aristocrats or those who have made lots of money with large houses and fast cars.

The Man in the Glass Booth

The following year, 1967, sees Pinter directing Robert Shaw's (1927–1978) *The Man in the Glass Booth* (1967) at the St. Martin's Theatre, London. In October 1968 Pinter directed the Broadway, New York production. In the Autumn of 1967 Pinter wrote *Landscape* for the Royal Shakespeare Company. The directing of Robert Shaw's work at this time may be seen as part of Pinter's retreat into a whirlwind of theatrical and other media activities as an escape from difficult disintegrating personal relationships with Vivien. Shaw's drama is a response to the Eichmann (1906–1962) trial in Jerusalem in 1961 in which one of the main exponents of the gas chambers was captured by Israeli agents in Argentina and secretly flown back to Israel to face trial and execution. The setting of Shaw's play is the trial of an extremely wealthy New Yorker masquerading as a former concentration camp guard. It raises questions to which Pinter is to return, most noticeably in *Reunion*, that is guilt and whether the Germans should be forgiven for their crimes. The drama and Pinter's involvement with it exhibits his concern with the Holocaust, dramatically expressed in what has been regarded by perceptive critics as his most moving, sensitive drama, *Ashes to Ashes* (1996).

Landscape, Silence, Night

Three short plays *Landscape*, *Silence* and *Night* (1969) constitute a natural evolution from Pinter's earlier dramatic work, yet a change from it to new departures. Following *The Homecoming*, Pinter confessed that he 'couldn't any longer stay in the room with this bunch of people who opened doors and came in and went out. *Landscape* and *Silence* are in a very different form. There isn't any menace at all' (cited Burkman, 1971: 141). Pinter cuts specific localising references, concentrating instead on compressed lyricism, going to the essence of his concerns, love, time, old age and memory itself. These plays 'offer cross-cut monologues' instead of verbal exchanges: they 'dispense with exits and entrances, [and] are distilled poetic evocations of separation and solitude. Pinter seems to be reaching out for a simpler, more direct form of theatre.' Billington adds that 'Emotionally [Pinter] was affected by the circumstances of his own life: the knowledge that marital happiness was increasingly becoming a distant memory' (*B*: 197).

Landscape

Landscape was mostly written near Stratford-upon-Avon in 1967. Somewhat ironically, it is dedicated to Vivien, who was performing in Peter Hall's production of *Macbeth* as Lady Macbeth at Stratford-upon-Avon. Its two characters are named 'Beth' and 'Duff' with the

'Mac' omitted. Vivien didn't perform the role of 'Beth' in either the BBC broadcast as a radio-play on 25 April 1968 or in the subsequent July 1969 stage performance by the Royal Shakespeare Company. The great actress Peggy Ashcroft (1907–1991) played Beth under Peter Hall's direction. Pinter recalls that the news that Vivien was not going to play the role deeply affected her: 'I think that had a great deal to do with the way our life together began to fall away . . . . Vivien was upset and I was equally upset that she could never bring herself to see the play onstage. It's a sign of the way our life had become a very thin thing by that time' (cited *B*: 201–202).

The play also ran into difficulties with the Lord Chamberlain's office to which all drama for stage performance still had to be submitted. At the censorship office, Charles D. Heriot commented on the script of *Landscape*: 'The nearer to Beckett, the more portentous Pinter gets . . . . Since there is very little shape, the thing just stops – rather like a contemporary serial musical composition. And of course, there have to be the ornamental indecencies.' He recommended the license for performance provided seven small cuts were made (cited Shellard, 2004: 171). His objections included a line such as 'Fuck all' (28). Such an attitude predictably provoked Pinter's anti-establishment, anti-authority sentiments and he refused to accept the cuts. However, by 1968 the Theatres Act abolished the censorship powers of the Lord Chamberlain's office and removed the obstacles to stage productions of *Landscape*.

Landscape is a poetic drama. The scenery is dominated by a kitchen table in a 'country house' on which 'a man in his early fifties' and 'a woman in her late forties' reflect upon their lives. The sky outside indicates 'Evening': the appropriate setting for the motif of mortality that reverberates throughout the play. In common with two musical voices, largely engrossed in their own separate thoughts, the counter point of the monologues of Duff and Beth create lyrical but discordant harmonies. As the stage direction indicates, 'Duff refers normally to Beth, but does not appear to hear her voice. Beth never looks at Duff, and does not appear to hear his voice. Both characters are relaxed, in no sense rigid' ([8]).

Beth dreams of men, birth and water. Duff, on the other hand, contemplates work, nature and people in general. He is fascinated by children, dogs, trees, ducks (which personally fascinate Pinter, too), rain, bread and small objects such as a bag. Occasionally, their thoughts co-mingle, for instance, when Beth moves from the beach and sea to think of birds, trees and the sun (21). Duff, too, moves from the external to the internal, however his thoughts are often crude: 'Mind you don't get the scissors up your arse' (29). The sudden vulgarity frequently provokes laughter in audiences, in what on the whole in common with its companion *Silence* are not Pinter plays noted for their humourous moments. Duff is able to transform the most mundane objects into lyrical ones. His experience as a cellarman, the beer, barrels, scissors and thimbles can take on a poetic quality. This element in Duff certainly emerges when he thinks of Beth: 'I stood close to you. Perhaps you were just thinking, in a dream. Without touching you, I could feel your bottom.'

Beth is a frustrated artist who 'remembered always, in drawing, the basic principles of shadow and light. Objects intercepting the light cast shadows. Shadow is deprivation of light' (27–28). She always seeks the light and the sun. These are not present in the 'dim . . . background' ([8]) in which the play takes place or in the masculine force she needs for completion and realisation of her fantasies. Her opening lines display her need for completion so evident throughout the play: 'I'll stand on the beach. On the beach. Well . . . it was very fresh. But it was hot, in the dunes. But it was so fresh, on the shore. I loved it very much . . . .. My man slept in the dune. He turned over as I stood. His eyelids. Belly button. Snoozing how lovely.' She has to ask the man for her final fulfilment: 'Would you like a baby? I said. Children? Babies? Of our own? Would be nice' ([9]). On the other hand, Duff finds his satisfaction in the nature around him. He reflects 'I should have some bread with me. I could have fed the birds' (11).

Beth's language is replete with the pronouns 'I', 'it', 'My', 'He', 'His'. They weigh her utterances with indefiniteness, with incompleteness at the very time she is trying to convince herself of the definiteness of her memories. There are times in which she appears to successfully reach beyond herself to other people from her dream-like world of memory. She wants to know whether or not other people are on the beach 'Did those women know me?' At times she participates in Duff's visions: 'There was an old man fiddling about on the cricket pitch, bending. I stood out of the sun, under a tree' (11, 21). There are flashes of recognition, of reality for Beth. There is 'plenty to be done and cleared up. I had put the plates in the sink to soak' (25) but these are intermittent flashes in a solipsistic, lyrical lament for the passing of beauty and a state of nostalgic frustration.

Landscape is limited to a particular scene and a specific land-scape. *Silence* belongs to the limitless universal. The play appeared on a double bill with *Landscape* and was first presented by the Royal Shakespeare Company at the Aldwich Theatre on 2 July 1969 directed by Peter Hall and followed the performance of *Landscape*. Harold Hobson in a very perceptive review of the first night appro-priately entitled 'Paradise Lost', comments 'In either play, the audience has to piece together into some sort of shifting coherence the fragmenting details of the partly recollected past, and in each case what is important is not the past, but the continuing influence that this past exercises on the present which is before our eyes on the stage' (*Sunday Times* 6 July 1969: 52).

Silence

For *Silence*, the stage direction reads 'Three areas. A chair in each area' ([32]) indicating an even more amorphous and non-naturalistic effect conjured up by the country house kitchen in *Landscape*. *Silence* finishes abruptly in the middle of a sentence which leaves only a 'Long silence' to confront the ears and the instruction to 'Fade lights' (51), to engage the eyes. The three characters in *Silence* are outside space and time with their chairs on a polished reflecting floor with their enlarged shadows for a period thrown back on the sloping surface of a sea increasingly threatening to engulf them. In other words, *Silence* deals with universals whereas *Landscape* is concerned with a particular marriage. In both plays and in *Night*, a Pinteresque silence takes on its own special meaning, indicating a longer rest than a pause in the ebb and flow of thought and emotion. These specific notations act as a controlling mechanism between the voices and indicate discordance or dissonance as well as harmony. For instance, Duff's 'Mmmnn?' is followed by a 'Pause' indicating a failure in communication (20–21).

According to Pinter, *Silence* 'took a long time to write – longer in fact than any full-length play of mine' (cited Hayman: 82). The text is replete with innumerable subtleties and nuances reading like an intricate and lyrical string trio with the sections marked by silences. There exist 29 of these divisions noted by 'Silence' and 14 'Pauses' which subside as the music develops. Structurally, there is a lengthy introductory section (33–35), then an opening movement of a somewhat similar length (35–39). The movements then get short, shorter and culminate in the long final silence and stage direction to 'Fade lights' (51). There are three stage directions that indicate movement: 'Bates moves to Ellen' (37); 'Ellen moves to Rumsey' (41) and this is repeated on page 44. The text of the play reveals close attention to textual typography, with attempts to create word or note blocks on the page of type, for instance, pages 41–42 contain woven patterns of short, sharp type blocks indicating Ellen and Rumsey's duet. Ellen's 'Does it get darker, the higher you get' precedes Rumsey's peremptory 'No' and that precedes a paragraph block of notes from Ellen (42–43). Non-capitalised words are used to begin a line, and lines are broken into separate halves.

Silence is permeated by individual memories of the past which all the characters attempt somehow to recreate in very beautiful lines. Bates' two lines 'From the young people's room – Silence. Sleep? Tender love?' find an answer in his blunt, 'It's of no importance' that conveys a sense of the infertility perceived by the three speakers. Ellen has an extended cadenza of memory that seems to speak for all of Pinter's characters: 'Yes, I remember. But I'm never sure that what I remember is of today or of yesterday or of a long time ago. And then often it is only half things I remember, half things, beginnings of things' (45–46). Such a vision of a world transcending a specific past pervades Pinter's next full-length drama *Old Times*.

Night

The seven page sketch *Night* is also extremely powerful. It was first performed in *Mixed Doubles* at the Comedy Theatre on 9 April 1969 with Vivien Merchant in the role of the woman and Nigel Stock (1919–1986), in the role of the man. The descriptions of the characters and stage directions are full of Pinteresque simplicity. 'A woman and a man in their forties. | They sit with coffee' ([54]). The play runs for 7 minutes and took only 40 minutes to write: 'I was sitting with my wife after lunch. Normally I fall asleep, but on this occasion I suddenly got up, went upstairs and wrote *Night*. It came so easily' (cited Hayman: 88). A man and a woman remember a moment by a river and how they made love by the railings. The man remembers; the woman confesses 'I can't remember.' His actions prompt the woman's memory. He put his 'hand on the small of your waist. Don't you remember? I put my hand under your coat.' They argue over the smallest details and in fact whether she was the woman the man was with. Ultimately, the experience was a very sensitive one and is expressed in superb poetry: 'You took my face in your hands, standing by the railings. You were very gentle, you were very caring. You cared. Your eyes searched my face. I wondered who you were. I wondered what you thought. I wondered what you would do' (55–56). The poetic effectiveness is conveyed through the cumulative 'w' sounds evoking her perception of wonder and fascination. *Night* concludes on a rare positive note. The woman says, 'And they said I will adore you always.' The man replies, 'Saying I will adore you always' (61).

The Go-Between

Pinter spent a good deal of time in 1969 and 1970, although there is an initial draft in the Pinter Archive at the British Library dating from 1964, working on the screenplay of *The Go-Between*. The film was shot during 1970, but not released owing to financial pressures until the following year. There was a star-studded cast with Julie Christie (1941–) as Marian and Alan Bates (1934–2003), who played Mick in the original production of *The Caretaker*, as Ted in the leading roles. Sir Michael Redgrave (1908–1985) was the old Leo Colston looking back on his life and the traumatic events that took place in 1900. Edward Fox (1937–) plays the role of the upper class Trimingham once in the running for Marian's affections and Margaret Leighton (1922–1976) as Mrs. Maudsley the seemingly all-knowing mother to Marian. The film was awarded the Cannes Film Festival Palmes d'Or, the British Film Academy Award for the Best Screenplay for 1971 and Margaret Leighton was nominated for an Academy Oscar for the Best Supporting Actress Performance. The film was a box office success on both sides of the Atlantic.

L. P. Hartley is a now unjustly neglected British writer. His novel punctuates a seemingly idyllic rural atmosphere with a tale of betrayal, intrigue, deception and the manipulation of others seen from the perspective of the past. *The Go-Between* is the tale of a young boy (Leo) caught in a love intrigue between two people from different classes that exhausts the limits of his understanding. The tale is told from his own very much older and wiser perspective. The film interweaves through flashbacks and voice-overs the distant past with the future. The idyllic dream landscape and the manipulation of memory, the inter-relationships of memory, time and change, become a dominant motif in Pinter's subsequent work.

Pinter compresses the action of Hartley's magnificent 281 page novel into a just less than 2-hour film. Brilliantly, Pinter remains faithful to the original and to his vision of its central preoccupation with mutability. Hartley uses a prologue and an epilogue in which the old Leo narrates his present feelings and his recently concluded trip to an ageing Marian in order to frame the real story. This concerns his role as the 'go-between' in the Ted–Marian relationship. Pinter compresses Leo's memories, his story into his later visit to an old Marian. Past and present, the old and the young, intermingle as does memory. He superimposes present voices on past actions and vice versa. In Pinter's version our perspective is shaped by that of the old Leo, in the novel Hartley retains the viewpoint of the young Leo except in the frame sections. Pinter's emphasis movingly juxtaposes innocence and experience. As Joseph Losey, the film's director, observes, 'there's a bitter core for those who can taste worm' (cited *Time* review, 9 August 1971: 45).

The young Leo comes into a world of private and public conflict, equipped with a public school ethic that tells him never to break a confidence and a boy's natural love of magic and secrecy. His innocence is accompanied by the belladonna motif and the summer heat that rises with the desires of Marian and Ted. Leo learns that love, too, can be a curse as mysterious as his own school curses. This knowledge which must remain secret affects him for the rest of his life. At the conclusion, the story disintegrates into a cloud of dust that arises from the expensive car that has brought the wealthy Leo, an old man, back into his distant past that has haunted his memories. The past climax is played out against the background of a superb house and beautiful countryside to which Pinter returns, for instance, in his early twenty-first century adaptation of Anthony Shaffer's (1926–2001), thriller *Sleuth*.

The Go-Between was filmed in the still relatively unspoiled Norfolk countryside and in Norwich. Passions, intrigue, class conflict, jealousy, rivalry, sexual ambiguity are brilliantly depicted at a cricket match. One of Hartley's subtexts is the Boer War (1899–1902) taking place in a far away country in which there are victims on both sides. Pinter removes these references in the novel: they are part of the adult world that the young Leo is unable to comprehend. The visual enactment of Ted's physical return to the scenes of his youth walking past a war memorial to the dead of the Boer War and the subsequent First World War in which Ted and many of the other cricketers and other spectators were slaughtered, not to mention another world war, is profoundly moving. Both novel and film open with Hartley's powerful, ironic sentence that echoes in the memory: 'The past is a foreign country. They do things differently there' (*The Go-Between*, 1965: 7; Pinter, *Five Screenplays*, 1971: [287]).

Old Times

According to Pinter, the idea for his next full-length play, *Old Times*, came to him at his Regent's Park house when he was reading a newspaper on a sofa one afternoon in the winter of 1970. *The Go-Between* had been shot and he was involved with directing James Joyce's *Exiles* (1918), at the Mermaid Theatre, London. This ran during the final months of 1970, Pinter's direction emphasised the significance of an apparently meaningless gesture, such as the removal of a pair of gloves, friendship and betrayal, the wounds of the past that never can be healed. These motifs are prominent in *Old Times*. *Old Times* opened at the Aldwych Theatre on 1 June 1971, directed for the Royal Shakespeare Company by Peter Hall to whom it is dedicated.

The reviews were ecstatic. Colin Blakely (1930–1987) played Deeley, Dorothy Tutin (1930–2001), Kate and Vivien Merchant, Anna. The three are 'All in their early forties.' The setting is 'A converted farmhouse.' It is 'Autumn. Night' ([6]). This first full-length Pinter play since *The Homecoming* returns to the conflict for dominance, possession and territory fought with the weaponry of innuendo and the ambiguous threat of his earlier drama. There is the return to the 'old times' of localised urban poetry combined with the new poetry of maximum compression and austerity found in *Landscape* and *Silence*. Deeley and his wife Kate await the visit of Anna, a friend whom Kate has not seen for 20 years. Anna intrudes and tries to interfere with the marriage of Deeley and Kate by attempting to recreate her close past friendship with Kate. Their relationship was severed by the intrusion of Deeley who now battles with Anna for possession of Kate.

The characters in *Old Times* don't belong to the world of the East End of London. Anna, for instance, if she is to be believed, is part of the jet set, of the Cote d'Azur, of what Deeley describes as 'Beautiful Mediterranean people . . . a kind of elegance we know nothing about, a slim-bellied Cote d'Azur thing we know absolutely nothing about, a lobster and lobster sauce ideology we know fuck all about.' Deeley is crude and ultimately submissive to Kate who tells him bluntly, 'If you don't like it go' (67). In keeping with later work, Pinter lets every word, even bits of clothing, take on significance. The words 'Mmnn' and 'Underwear' (9–10) are said by Kate early in the play and already raise questions about her possible relationship with Anna. Deeley's hostility to Anna emerges after this initial mention of underwear. The play is replete with beautiful, lyrical recall. Like Duff in *Landscape*, Deeley remembers 'Sometimes I take her face in my hands and look at it' (24). Kate enjoys 'living close to the sea too. You can't say where it begins or ends' (59). Deeley remembers Kate's face in his hands only to 'kind of let it go, take my hands away, leave it floating . . . it just floats away' (24).

The play is full of pauses and silences. Ronald Bryden in a review in *The Observer* (6 June 1971), of the first night, notes the way in which Peter Hall directed 'with a musician's ear for the value of each word and silence' (27). Particularly striking was Vivien Merchant's pause before she replied to Deeley's 'Do you drink brandy?' Her pause prior to responding 'I would love some brandy' (18) is, Bryden writes, 'just sufficient to remind you that on Pinter territory, every question is an attempt to control and every answer a swift evasion' (27). Pinter moreover, more so than in any other of his plays, uses song lyrics and music by, in this instance, Jerome Kern (1885–1945), George Gershwin (1898–1937), and Richard Rogers (1902–1979), and Lorenz Hart (1895–1943), to evoke nostalgia and the memory of past relationships. Deeley's recall of 'You're lovely to look at, delightful to know' is tempered by Anna's recall of 'Smoke gets in your eyes.' Such song lyrics provide a running commentary and combine to convey a powerful sense of the past, of memories, of what has now gone forever (27–29).

If the ghosts of Billie Holiday (1915–1959), singing such great melodies haunt the farm house setting of *Old Times*, so do the memories of a London of 20 years previously. Deeley remembers that he and Anna 'met in the Wayfarers Tavern. In the corner. She took a fancy to me.' He tells Kate that Anna was 'Wearing your underwear she was too, at the time . . . . We went to a party. Given by philosophers. Not a bad bunch. Edgware Road gang' (69). One of the most memorable moments of *Old Times* is found in Anna's recollection of 'Queuing all night, the rain, do you remember? my goodness, the Albert Hall, Covent Garden, what did we eat? to look back, half the night, to do things we loved, we were young then of course, but what stamina, and to work in the morning' (17). The London of her youth has dissipated as has her youth. London has changed because she has changed: 'but of course there was so much, so much to see and to hear, in lovely London then' (38).

Old Times is one of Pinter's most Proustian attempts at memories of things past. The memories in *Old Times* of popular songs and films of the 1940s function as an attempt to capture the past, a past that is gone forever and can be only occasionally and imperfectly recaptured. In the present, as Deeley says, 'We rarely get to London' (18) but it remains the location for the memory of happy events and sexual experience. The close intermingling of past and present in the mind of Deeley is found, for instance, in his remembering watching '*Odd Man Out* and thought Robert Newton was fantastic. And I still think he was fantastic. And I would commit murder for him, even now' (29). The mixed tenses reveal Deeley's attempt to make the past real in the present. Deeley's memory of the 1947 *Odd Man Out* film displays his Irishness and has contemporary significance to the early 1970s. This is a period of the particularly intensive and prolonged IRA bombing campaign on the British mainland. Carol Reed's 1947 film is a moving cinematic impression of the final hours of a IRA gunman on the run in an unknown city being hunted down and killed. James Mason gave a powerful depiction of the hunted, haunted gunman.

Old Times focuses on sexual and personal memories, but political references, too, act as an undercurrent. The play carries a direct message about the world of the early 1970s. London and its activities appear not to have changed. The Promenade concerts, the opera, the theatre continue. Mini skirts have eased the task of looking up girls skirts. Yet a direct contemporary political note enters overtly, not merely as an allusion to the title of a 1947 film. Deeley is afraid of China, of 'China *and* death' and 'the stinking breath and their broken teeth and the hair in their noses and China and death and their arses' (51). This is a memory of a Wayfarers Tavern argument of 20 years previously. The Russians then were the enemy, in the early 1970s they are transformed into the Chinese. During the late 1960s and early 1970s, the violence and horror of the Cultural Revolution was seeping even into the television screens of London pubs, along with news of the Reuters man, Anthony Grey (1938–), held captive in Beijing.

Old Times, points to earlier Pinter plays in its treatment of a conflict, the power struggle for dominance and possession. Its economy of poetic significance indicates a subsequent phase of Pinter's work. The overt intrusion of politics also points forward to subsequent Pinter preoccupations. Above all, *Old Times* is haunted by memory and time, an obsession that remains with Pinter.

Chapter Six
The 1970s and 1980s

The 1970s

Langrishe, Go Down

Pinter started the decade of the 1970s wrestling with the adaptation of Aiden Higgins' novel *Langrishe, Go Down*. This was first written as a screenplay in 1971, the rights were held in the USA and the film was never made, but was produced for the BBC TV in 1978, directed by David Jones (1934–), who also directed the film version of *Betrayal*, and broadcast on 20 September 1978. It serves as a prelude to Pinter's struggle with his adaptation of Marcel Proust's great novel *À la Recherche du Temps Perdu*. Higgins' novel is more than being merely about three unmarried sisters living in a large dilapidated old house during the 1930s in the middle of Ireland and their relationship with a German student, played by Jeremy Irons, who rents their lodge. The film focuses upon memories, fantasy, the past, the erotic and Ireland. For Pinter, it marks a sort of return to the country. The film was shot in the Waterford area where 28 years previously Pinter had performed in *Othello* at the Theatre Royal. The film and the novel are also about drink, drunkenness and virginity. In other words, about what might have been. Above all, it is about the past and present, and Pinter's own personal tribute to the Ireland he had known in the early 1950s.

The depiction of the German student explores the complexity of the German character. This is a theme Pinter is subsequently to return to in his adaptation of Fred Uhlman's *Reunion*. Aiden Higgins prefaces his *Helsing for Station – Other Departures Fiction and Autobiographies 1956–1989* (1989) with an unattributed

Richard Jefferies (1848–1887) citation: 'The ghosts die as we grow older, they die and their places are taken by real ghosts . . . the happiest days become the saddest afterwards; let us never go back, lest we too die.' These lines from Walter Besant's *The Eulogies of Richard Jefferies* (1882: 42) refer to Coate Farmhouse where Jefferies grew up. The ironic ambiguity and sadness and attempt to return to childhood are brilliantly evoked, as we have seen, in Pinter's adaptation of *The Go-Between* and above all, *The Proust Screenplay* which he worked on obsessively with Joseph Losey and Barbara Bray, the distinguished translator and close friend of Samuel Beckett.

The Proust Screenplay

Much of Pinter's time during the early 1970s was preoccupied with his adaptation of Marcel Proust's novel as a screenplay. It remained un-filmed but was published as *The Proust Screenplay* in 1982. A collaborative work, Pinter became totally obsessed by, for instance, the idea of an opening montage of 35 shots before a word is spoken. Many perceptive commentators such as Billington regard *The Proust Screenplay* 'in its published form . . . [as] one of Pinter's most extraordinary achievements: an act of homage by one artist to another' (*B*: 225). Until the very last line of the film script, there is no use of external narration, with no voice-over. In other words, nothing comes between the viewer and the event. In his introduction to the published text, Pinter emphasises the dual momentum of the novel which deals on the one hand with the disintegration of French society between around 1880 and 1919 and the private disenchantment of Marcel, the central consciousness. 'The subject was Time . . . Marcel, in his forties hears the bell of his childhood. His childhood, long forgotten, is suddenly present within him, but his consciousness of himself as a child, his memory of the experience, is more real, more acute than the experience itself' (viii). This motif Pinter had previously explored, for instance, in *The Go-Between*. Of course, memory is unreliable and ambiguous, forever an enigma. Pinter's 'screenplay was based on a chain of visual and aural motifs, and interlocking images' (*B*: 231). The film was not made and its first production was as a sound broadcast on BBC Radio 3 in December 1995, with Pinter as the interlinking narrator.

As Pinter said in his 'Introduction' to the printed text, 'Working on *À la Recherche du Temps Perdu* was the best working year of my life' (viii). Indeed, it was both a journey of discovery and in a way his own homecoming revealing a multitude of selves contained within the single individual. He also became fully aware of the sharpness of sensory impression experienced during childhood, and the ability of memory to operate on many different levels. These subsequently become preoccupations in his work, although they were present previously. For Billington, the encounter with Proust encouraged Pinter's 'experiments with time and memory, and to drive him further away from a narrow representational realism.' Pinter became convinced even more of 'the absolute integrity of art' and it reinforced his awareness of the issue of whether art 'can also be detached from a social and political purpose' (*B*: 233).

No Man's Land

Time, allusion, political satire and power play based in Hollywood, combined with the mixing of dreams and reality, dominate Pinter's screenplay of F. Scott Fitzgerald's *The Last Tycoon*. Commissioned by Sam Spiegel (1901–1985), the distinguished American independent film producer, and directed by Elia Kazan (1909–2003), Pinter spent most of 1974 on the adaptation. The film released 3 years later was not well received. While wrestling with this adaptation, an image or a mood came to Pinter to form the foundation for his drama *No Man's Land*, completed on 11 September 1974. Dedicated to his manager Jimmy Wax and directed by Peter Hall, it was first presented by the National Theatre at the Old Vic on 23 April 1975. There are no female characters and four male leads: 'Hirst, a man in his sixties' played by Sir Ralph Richardson (1902–1983); 'Spooner, a man in his sixties' played by Sir John Gielgud (1904–2000); 'Foster, a man in his thirties' and 'Briggs, a man in his forties' ([7]). These are all named after pre-1914 First World War cricketers, two of whom, Hirst and Spooner, competed against each other as they do in the play. Peter Hall in his *Diaries* encapsulates the themes of the play, focusing upon 'opposites. Genius against lack of talent, success against failure, [drink] against sobriety, elegance against uncouthness, smoothness against roughness, politeness against violence.' Billington adds that one could easily add to this list 'fixity against flux, past against present, memory against reality, town against country' (246).

The setting is not the East End but 'A large room in a house in North West London' ([9]). There are two servants with whom Spooner is constantly engaged in a power battle. There are two acts. Act I takes place in 'Summer' and 'Night' ([13]). The second act in the 'Morning' ([57]). The play is poetic and bleak, with memory stirred by photographs of the dead and the constant need to go to the drinks cabinet. The play's success was reinforced by the particularly powerful, evocative performance of Sir John Gielgud in the role of Spooner that stole the show.

monologue

One of the most neglected, powerful and revealing of Pinter plays is *monologue*. It was written in the early 1970s and presented on the BBC-2 TV on 13 April 1973. Pinter's old childhood friend, Henry Woolf, played the role of the 'Man', the only character in a play containing powerful poetic passages. A pugnacious solitary figure, 'alone in a chair' refers 'to another chair, which is empty' ([7]). He speaks either to his memories or imagines other people sitting in the other chair. The play is replete with lists frequently found in Pinter's work. Recalling his youth he says to the chair, 'You haven't forgotten *me*. Who was your best mate, who was your truest mate? You introduced me to Webster and Tourneur, admitted, but who got you going on Tristran Tzara, Breton, Giacommetti and all that lot? Not to mention Louis-Ferdinand Celine, now out of favour. And John Dos.' Surrealist artists are juxtaposed with a French fascist collaborationist writer Celine – a writer who was himself obsessed with the idea of betrayal – and a left-wing American experimental writer, John Dos Passos who subsequently renounced the Communist sympathies of his youth. These are followed by a highly suggestive sexual allusion, typical of Pinter who moves from the cerebral to the sensual and vulgar almost in one breath: 'Who bought you both [whoever the plural may refer to] all those custard tins cut price?' ([11–12]). This is hilariously funny and yet very serious, given the juxtapositions moving from Jacobean dramatists bent on revenge, to collaborationist and experimental authors, then to erotic innuendo.

The few who have discussed *monologue* 'a work of only 1,253 words', tend to perceive it as a pessimistic vision. Linda Ben-Zvi writing, for instance, in her '*Monologue*: The Play of Words' that 'With economy Pinter describes a world with no future, only the past linguistically replayed over and over in the present. Even a count of the verb tenses in *monologue* illustrates the situation: 48 are past tense, 18 present and only six future' (81, 85). The sexual and intellectual allusions are in the past. However, not all is bleak: the play ends on a note of positive affirmation with the words 'I love your children' whoever 'your' ([19]) may refer to. Revived in performances by Henry Woolf at the South Bank in 2001, reasons for the neglect of this important work containing the quintessence of Pinter, his obsession with the past, fantasy, erotic memory, conflict, time, class, social status and much more, might lie in the text's relative inaccessibility. It was published by the now long defunct Covent Garden Press in a limited signed edition of 100 copies and an ordinary standard one of just under 2,000 copies. Subsequently, it was reprinted in Eyre Methuen's *Plays Four* (1981). Pinter dedicated these memories of his youthful fantasies to his son Daniel.

Lady Antonia Fraser

This whirlwind of creative activity was paralleled by tremendous transformations in Pinter's personal life. Technically, he was still married to Vivien Merchant. In 1969 he briefly met Antonia Fraser, the distinguished writer of historical biographies. They re-met a few years later in January 1970 and again in January 1975 at a revival of *The Birthday Party*. According to Pinter, 'We fell in love instantly and have remained just as strongly in love over all the years that have passed' (cited *B*: 252). Many of Pinter's most moving poems have been love poems to Antonia, celebrating their love. For instance, when they first met they went together to Paris. Pinter celebrates this in a two verse poem of four lines each concluding 'She dances in my life. | The white day burns' (*VV*: 159). In 'I know the place', which also belongs to 1975, he writes 'Everything we do | Corrects the space | Between death and me | And you' (160). In 'Poem' written in June 2007 and included in *Six Poems for A* (2007), the apotheosis of their relationship is celebrated in a simple, heartfelt, powerful line 'I miss you when I am dead.'

Pinter left home and Vivien on 28 April 1975, five days after the first night of *No Man's Land*. A broken, distraught Vivien gave sensational press interviews: 'It seems' she told William Hickey in the *Daily Express*, 'he is possessed by Lady Antonia – she has cast a spell on him. How can she do it with six children to look after I don't know' (cited *B*: 254). Pinter and Antonia went into hiding. Vivien sued for divorce. Daniel their son came to live with Pinter and Lady Antonia although he changed his name at this time from Pinter to Brand, using Vivien's grandmother's maiden name. Lady Antonia's six children from her first marriage have themselves produced 17 grandchildren who call Pinter 'Grandpa' (cited Sarah Lyall Interview, the *New York Times*, 'Art and Leisure', October 7, 2007: 16).

In October 1980, Pinter and Antonia married. She was the wife of a Conservative MP, the daughter of a Labour Peer, from the Catholic aristocracy, wealthy and exceedingly well-connected socially, apart from being a highly successful writer in her own right. Very politically committed on the left, she openly encouraged what till they met had been largely dormant, her husband's political left-wing activism and fully participated in all his activities, including, for instance, his involvement with Anthony Astbury and the Greville Press. Pinter and Astbury, a preparatory school master and poet based in Warwick, met in 1975 when the latter invited Pinter to give a reading of his poems in Warwick. Pinter, Lady Antonia and Astbury had common poetic tastes. For instance, they both consider W. S. Graham and George Barker (1913–1991) to be highly significant poets. The press was begun with readings by poets at the Purcell Room on the South Bank in September 1979. Pinter has co-edited two anthologies, *100 Poems by 100 Poets* (1986) and *99 Poems in Translation* (1994). Pinter has financed over 20 volumes of poetry published by the press, including his own and Lady Antonia's work and selections from others, for instance, *Poems by Philip Larkin* (2002).

These publications contain some of the most revealing and interesting indications of Pinter's own taste and writings and are collectors items having been published only in limited editions.

Betrayal

Betrayal (1977) is the first play Pinter wrote following the breakup with Vivien and his going to live with Lady Antonia. It is dedicated to the dramatist Simon Gray (1936–) whose *Butley* was directed by Pinter in 1971 in Oxford and London, and 2 years later on the BBC Television. Pinter directed three more of Gray's plays. *Betrayal* opened at the National Theatre in November 1978 with Penelope Wilton in the role of Emma, Michael Gambon as Jerry and Daniel Massey (1933–1998) as Robert, under Peter Hall's direction and designed by John Bury (1925–2000). Pinter has been remarkably loyal to his directors, designers and actors. Penelope Wilton, Michael Gambon and Jeremy Irons have frequently appeared in his cinematic adaptations, readings and revivals of his work. David Jones directed the film version in the early 1980s and it was released in 1983 with Jeremy Irons, Patricia Hodge (1946–) and Ben Kingsley (1943–) in the leading roles. Jones tells the story that he and Pinter wanted Helen Mirren (1945–) to cinematically play the leading female role. Sam Spiegel the producer of the film asked her to walk down the corridor to go to lunch as he, Pinter and Jones followed. He then told them that she was far too sensuous for the part and would distract from the other elements in the film! So Helen Mirren must be one of the few actresses who did not get a role because the producer found her back view too attractive for the part she would have been performing (Jones discussion, 'Viva Pinter', Lyons, 24 March 2007).

The film was filmed on location in the actual house in West London in Kilburn where Harold Pinter and the TV presenter and journalist Joan Bakewell had in fact carried out an affair lasting from 1962 to 1969. Bakewell was well known to television viewers of a certain generation as she presented late night television arts programmes. She received the supreme accolade in the popular press of the mid-1970s being described as 'the thinking man's crumpet'. At the time of their affair, both she and Pinter were married to others. *Betrayal* is the tale of an emotional triangle centred on human insecurities and personal betrayals of friends. Bakewell was married to the producer Michael Bakewell who helped Pinter in his earlier years and adapted subsequently in 1995 his *Proust Screenplay* as a 2-hour radio-play. Joan Bakewell returned to her husband following her affair with Pinter and has written without recrimination about her relationship with Pinter in her autobiography *The Centre of the Bed* (2003).

As Proust, *Betrayal* is obsessed with time and memory. Billington cites Joan Bakewell as saying 'the nature of memory is very important to' Pinter and she quotes him as saying 'Isn't it interesting that one tries to remember something and one isn't sure that it happened exactly like that?' (265). *Betrayal* presents in reverse replay an affair lasting for 7 years between a literary agent, Jerry, and Emma, the wife of his best friend, a publisher. Betrayals, personal and professional, permeate the drama whether in the form of the betrayal of the lofty ideals of youth or even of children. There is a coherent structure which goes back 9 years: time is presented backward. The text starts in 1977, then moves to 1975, then to 1974, then to 1973, then 1971 and finally to 1968. The characters are upper middle-class intellectuals and Pinter reveals the way in which memory, the mind and relationships operate by playing with time and recall. The film allows Pinter to introduce children and how (as in *The Go-Between*) they too become caught in a spider's web of intrigue and lies played out by adults. Children's sense of something happening is conveyed via a telephone call. The children want to know who is on the phone. Emma tells them that daddy sends his love. What she says is accurate, but she has omitted that it is someone else who rings and doesn't necessarily send the children his love. In short, *Betrayal* has corrosive consequences.

Pinter doesn't pass moral judgement on human activity. There is deliberate ambiguity in *Betrayal* and in his other work. The film version, which he wrote between 21 April 1981 and 2 March 1982 allows him to show the children as they get younger, some of them aren't born at its beginning, to pare down his original stage drama, and to add three new scenes mostly involving exteriors. For instance, Robert sits in a BMW car watching Jerry's flat, thus creating a sense of foreboding. Also Robert discovers the affair while he and Emma holiday in Venice. She misplaces a letter she has written to Jerry. In another scene, Robert collects one of the children – Ned, who is in fact his child, although ambiguity had previously been created concerning whether the child was his or Jerry's. The film concludes as it began with the exterior of Robert and Emma's home. A party is going on inside. Jerry and Emma's hands intertwine. Gale observes, 'All of the passion and betrayals, the ironies, loss, and sadness of the story are captured emotionally in this last shot and freeze frame' (*Sharp Cut*, 2003: 271).

The French Lieutenant's Woman

Between 1978 and May 1980 Pinter worked on the adaptation of John Fowles' novel *The French Lieutenant's Woman* (1969). Pinter recalled that 'The problems involved in transposing' the novel 'to film are quite considerable. It pretends to be a Victorian novel, but it isn't. It's a modern novel, and it's made clear by the author that he's writing it now. The whole idea had to be retained' (Gussow, *Conversations*, 1994: 53). One of the ways in which the world of 1867 and the present, both depicted in the novel, are juxtaposed in Pinter's film script cinematically is through parallels between the lives of the fictional characters Charles and Sarah and the lives of the contemporary actors, Mike and Anna who are playing them. Both have partners whom they betray. In Mike's case, he betrays also his children in his web of deceit and intrigue. The idea for this was not Harold Pinter's but Karel Reisz (1926–2002) the film's director. Building upon his suggestion, Pinter uses dialogue, scene changes and cross-cutting 'by replacing the narrator with a twentieth-century story line and developing a film-within-film structure' (*Sharp Cut*: 242). Two realities are created, that of the present and of the past, bringing them close together while being simultaneously distinct. Such a technique allows Pinter to show differences in attitudes. For instance, in the twenty-seventh shot, Mike and Anna are sleeping together in her hotel room. The telephone rings and is answered by Mike. The film unit has rung to say that Anna is late for filming. She objects to Mike taking the call: 'They'll fire me for immorality. They'll think I'm a whore' (*The Screenplay of The French Lieutenant's Woman*, 1982: 9) she says jokingly and ironically as a contemporary feminist. For Sarah Woodruff however in 1857, she is haunted by an apparent sexual relationship with a Frenchman who has deserted her. She tells Charles 'I have set myself beyond the pale. I am nothing. I am hardly human any more. I am the French Lieutenant's Whore' (45).

Pinter's film adaptation which reduces a very lengthy novel with alternative endings to around 2 hours cinematic running time, received highly favourable reviews and an Academy Award nomination for the Best Film for 1981. Meryl Streep (1949–) for her performance as Sarah and Anna received the Best Actress nomination. Commercially, the film was a box office success. The East End of Pinter's earlier years and work seems far away. There is, however, Sam, Charles's cockney manservant with his own commercial dreams, wishing to go into business: 'Drapers and haberdashers. I've set my heart on a little shop' (66). He is not beyond potential blackmail to achieve his ends. The modern setting of the novel is not the East End of London but greener pastures, the film's location at Lyme Regis in Dorset and Mike's expensive Victorian London house, with its garden large enough to accommodate a 'three-piece band on a platform' (103) and the cast and crew of the film for a farewell party. There have been shots, brief ones of the seedier sides of central London in Victorian times as Charles searches the London streets in vain for Sarah. She is eventually found drawing at an expensive house on Lake Windermere, not in the London slums or brothels. In short, Pinter's adaptation of Fowles's superb fiction is largely removed from his previous worlds. Pinter's obsession is now with time, with the past and the present: the film adaptation took 'over a year' to write (xvi). It is moving, real and yet dream-like. Collaboratively, with superb direction and acting, it is one of Pinter's most powerful achievements.

The 1980s

In retrospect, the 1980s were a very creative active period for Pinter. He was involved in at least eight film adaptations and five of his own dramas in addition to directing on the London stage. On a personal level, on 3 October 1982, 11 days before the opening, at the Cottesloe

Theatre on the South Bank, of *Other Places* as a triple bill consisting of *A Kind of Alaska*, *Victoria Station* and *Family Voices* directed by Peter Hall for the Royal National Theatre, Vivien Merchant died. Her death coincides with a creative hiatus for Pinter.

Family Voices

Family Voices was written in 1980, broadcast on BBC Radio 3 in January 1981 and then in a platform performance by the National Theatre on 13 February 1981. The director for the broadcast and performance was Peter Hall. It consists of three voices. The first was performed by Michael Kitchen (1948–), the second by Peggy Ashcroft and the third by Mark Dignam (1909–1989). The play focuses upon families seen through the lens of memory and recollection, a reliving of sexual longing, betrayal, love between fathers and sons, a son's relationship with his mother. These fundamentally serious concerns are comically depicted among a collection of idiosyncratic characters. There is a 'landlady, Mrs. Withers' who apparently 'was in the Women's Air Force in the Second World War. Don't drop a bollock, Charlie, she's fond of saying, Call him Flight Sergeant and he'll be happy as a pig in shit' (*Other Places*: *Three Plays*, 1982: 69).

Victoria Station

Victoria Station, the second of the three pieces constituting *Other Places*, harks back to Pinter's earlier review sketches. It is concerned with two characters unable to communicate with one another, although ironically they are in voice contact. The Controller of a radio-cab business is vainly attempting to tell a lonely driver how to get to Victoria Station. The play is both very funny and very sad, place names such as the Barbados, Boulogne, Cuckfield and Crystal Palace intermingle with explosions of coarse frustration from the Controller. He tells the unseen driver 'it'll be nice to meet you in the morning. I'm really looking forward to it.' Violence, not without its humorous side, then intrudes: 'I'll be sitting here with my cat o' nine tails, son. And you know what I'm going to do with it? I'm going to tie you up, bollock naked to a butcher's table and I'm going to flog you to death, all the way to Crystal Palace.' This evokes the response from the driver 'That's where I am! I knew I knew the place' (54) – words echoed in the title of Pinter's poems, *I Know the Place* (1979) and his poem to Antonia dated 1975, 'I Know the Place.' The sadness in *Victoria Station* is reinforced with the realisation that the driver has lost it. Asked if he'd ever heard of Victoria Station, he replies, 'Never. No' and confesses, 'I honestly don't know what I've been doing all these years.' The Controller asks him, 'What have you been doing all these years?' The reply is, 'Well, I honestly don't know' (53). The Controller too admits his frailty to the unseen voice somewhere in the urban wilderness: 'I think I'm going to die. I'm alone in this miserable freezing fucking office and nobody loves me' (58). The play ends with the Controller leaving the office and going to actually, apparently be with the driver.

A Kind of Alaska

Forgetfulness and sleep are the themes of the finest of the three plays. *A Kind of Alaska* (1982) 'was inspired' by Pinter's reading of Dr. Oliver Sacks *Awakenings* (1973). This is a medical account of 20 patients who 'erupted into life once more' following 'the development of the remarkable drug L-DOPA' 50 years after the winter of 1916–1917. During this period, there spread a worldwide 'epidemic illness which presented itself in innumerable forms – as delirium, mania, trances, coma, sleep, insomnia, restlessness and states of Parkinsonism.' During the following 'ten years almost five million people fell victim to the disease of whom more than a third died. Of the survivors, some escaped almost unscathed, but the majority moved into states of deepening illness.' *A Kind of Alaska* based on Sacks account, focuses on the eruption into life again of 'the worst-affected', those who 'sunk into singular states of "sleep" – conscious of their surroundings but motionless, speechless, and without hope or will, confined to asylums or other institutions' ([v]).

In the Cottesloe auditorium National Theatre performances of *A Kind of Alaska*, the three who have come to life again are Deborah, played by Judi Dench (1934–), Hornby, by Paul Rogers (1917–), the original Max in *The Homecoming*, and Pauline, by Anna Massey

(1937–). Pinter's creative transformation reflects the themes of Sacks account. Pinter first read *Awakenings* when it was published in 1973 and 'He had been deeply moved; but . . . he had then "forgotten" it and that it had stayed "forgotten" until it suddenly came back to him years later.' According to Sacks account of a 1982 letter Pinter sent him, which he recalls in a revised edition of *Awakenings* published in 1990, 'Pinter had awoken, he said, one morning the previous summer, with the first image of the play – the patient awakening – and the first words of the play ("Something is happening") clear and pressing in his mind; and the play had then "written itself" in the days and weeks that followed' (cited *B*: 281).

Deborah awakes aged 45, having been 'asleep' for 29 years. For Deborah, the past is her present. This is contrasted with the present, the immediate world of Doctor Hornby who has affectionately looked after her, and the world of her sister Pauline, married to Hornby. The two worlds of time and memory movingly coexist, but are not the same: there is the dream and the reality. This is powerfully, poetically conveyed in memories, of what has actually transpired in the real world over the years during Deborah's 'sleep' (7) and in Judi Dench's great performance as Deborah.

Precisely and *One for the Road*

The plays which followed, *Precisely* and *One for the Road* (1984), are politically inspired after a period of around 3 years in which Pinter didn't write a play. *Precisely* is a short sketch written and directed by Pinter as part of the 5-hour anti-nuclear gala, *The Big One*, arranged by the actress and political activist Susannah York (1942–) and Bill Blanche, which opened at the Apollo Victoria Theatre, London on 18 December 1983. *One for the Road*, first performed at the Lyric Theatre Studio, Hammersmith in March 1984 directed by Pinter, deals not with the horrors of nuclear war, but with the abuse of human rights and focuses upon power and powerlessness. It is Pinter's response to the widespread use of torture in Turkey to suppress the opposition to the regime on the part of writers and other artists, intellectuals, racial minorities and peace campaigners. In March 1985 with the great American dramatist Arthur Miller (1915–2005) in their official positions as Vice-Presidents of English and American

PEN, Pinter and Miller spent 5 days in Turkey to witness the situation first-hand. Pinter lost his temper at a dinner party given by the Ambassador of the United States. The next morning, he and Miller left the country.

Pinter's political activism was also expressed in his participation in public protests outside, for instance, the American Embassy in London in February 1987 against the United States actions in Nicaragua. He also signed petitions, took part in interviews, wrote letters and articles drawing attention, for instance, to the condemnation by the International Court of Justice in June 1986 of the United States actions in Nicaragua, its overthrowing of democratic governments in Guatemala in 1954 and in Chile in 1973. On 20 June 1986, he and Antonia began participating in regular meetings of a group of like-minded left-wing liberals. They came to be known as the June 20th Society. The group disbanded in 1992.

Mountain Language

Moreover, Pinter, following his Turkish visit, became increasingly aware of the perilous situation of the roughly 15 million Kurdish minorities in Turkey. Their plight led to his writing *Mountain Language*. Dedicated to Antonia, this was first performed at the National Theatre on 20 October 1988 and directed by Pinter himself. The eight persons in this very short play lack names and have merely general titles. There is a 'Young Woman', an 'Elderly Woman', a 'Sergeant', an 'Officer', a 'Guard', a 'Prisoner', a 'Hooded Man' and a 'Second Guard' ([9]). A succinct note on the front flap of the dust jacket of the text of *Mountain Language* reads, 'The play consists of a series of images on the theme of language and oppression.' The motifs of menace, persecution, uncertainty, power games against the vulnerable, betrayals and the loss of language, are its preoccupation. While the Kurds were the inspiration for the play, its language, its expressions are English. Pinter told Anna Ford during a BBC TV interview that: 'I'm not writing a play simply about Turkey.' He adds, 'in fact the play isn't about Turkey at all. I think the play is very much closer to home and I believe it reflects a great deal what's happening in this country' (Smith, 2005: 86).

Set in an unspecified location where 'mountain people' live and are separated from those living in 'the capital', their language 'is forbidden', they are forbidden to speak it and 'may only speak the language of the capital' (21). There are four scenes set around a prison camp. In the first, women wait outside to visit their men. An older woman is bitten by a dog and a young woman who according to a Sergeant 'looks like a fucking intellectual to me', is harassed by the Sergeant and Officer. The former also commenting 'Intellectual arses wobble the best' (25). The following three scenes are brief and take place inside the prison. In the second, the older woman visits her son. She is unable to speak the language of the capital. The audience hears their thoughts, their 'voice'. The third scene depicts the conse-quent punishment for not speaking the correct language. Accidentally, the young woman encounters her husband hooded, probably awaiting torture. They briefly reminisce, the lights come up on stage and he collapses. The woman tries to bargain with the Sergeant.

The repetitive four letter word is characteristic of this stage of Pinter's work, expressing the paucity, the breakdown in *Mountain Lan-guage* of language itself. The young woman asks the Sergeant 'Can I fuck him? If I fuck him, will everything be alright?' (41): this is a very moving plea replete with pathos and powerlessness. The fourth scene returns to the Mother and her son of the second scene. Now apparently the rules have changed, and they are allowed to use their own mountain language. The Mother remains silent, unable in spite of her son's pleas to suggest anything. In the final lines of the play, the Sergeant has no sympathy for the son who collapses and physically begins 'to gasp and shake violently'. The Sergeant has the final word saying to the accompa-nying guard, 'Look at this. You go out of your way to give them a helping hand and they fuck it up' (47). Language is crucial to the play, as a tool of aggression and silence, perhaps resistance. Verbal assaults and abuse are found in Pinter's earlier plays, but in *Mountain Language* the characters are not as developed as say Goldberg in *The Birthday Party* or Mick in *The Caretaker*. Silence on the other hand can be sub-mission, powerlessness or can even denote resistance.

Sweet Bird of Youth

Pinter's political involvement during the 1980s is also reflected in the plays he chose to direct and the films he chose to adapt. For instance, in July 1985, he directed Tennessee Williams's (1911–1983) *Sweet Bird of Youth* (1959) at the Theatre Royal, Haymarket. Pinter's revival of the play attracted attention as Lauren Bacall (1924–) played the role of the once famous movie queen. Pinter's emphasis, however, was rather focused towards the often neglected political aspect of the play and particularly its author's attack on racism and homophobia, depicted in the powerful scenes in which the gigolo-hero is castrated by Southern redneck bullies.

Victory

The seven films Pinter adapted during this period also have a political element. The first is *Victory* based on Joseph Conrad's novel published in 1915. Pinter comments in the published version 'I wrote *Victory* in 1982, working with the director, Richard Lester [1932–]. The finance for the film was never found' (166). The narrative has much in common with Pinter's other work, with intruders, corruption, destiny, death and ambiguity. Conrad's title is deeply ambiguous – whose 'victory'? – certainly not of the isolated Heyst and the young violinist Lena he rescues. They are hounded by villains who are destroyed. Heyst sets his own home on fire, while he holds onto the dead Lena. Conrad's vision is nihilistic. Pinter truncates the novel, uses flashbacks used by Conrad yet doesn't reveal crucial information. In some instances, narrative is replaced by dialogue and actual events taking place to reveal the punctuation of dreams and illusions. At the conclusion of Conrad's novel, the narrator relates the house burning and Heyst holding Lena's dead body amidst the flames. Pinter's script shows the actual flames. In political terms, the novel and screenplay explore the use and abuse of male-dominated power and the abortive attempt to escape, to retreat from the real world into an illusory one of dreams.

Turtle Diary

Pinter's next film adaptation is the 1975 novel *Turtle Diary* by the American writer Russell Hoban (1925–). Told from differing points of view, *Turtle Diary* is an account of William Snow who works in a bookshop and Neaera Duncan who writes children's books, and their attempt to rescue three giant sea turtles that have lived in the London Zoo aquarium for 30 years. Written largely during 1984, the film was released in 1985. It is the tale of lonely people who through a cause come together and free themselves from their own entrapment. The distinguished film cast included Glenda Jackson (1936–) and Ben Kingsley in the leading roles, with Pinter himself playing the small role of a man in a bookshop. The film was a commercial success. There are scenes depicting everyday reality, for instance, an old man and woman taking their dog for a walk. In other words, little basic everyday details of life as it is lived, are depicted. The film and the novel work on many levels: as a comment on animal rights and the environment, personal entrapment and sharing through a cause, the creation of a new life and death. Such motifs are brilliantly revealed in the film through the use of dominating sea and water imagery.

Reunion

Pinter's mother recommended Fred Uhlman's 1971 novella *Reunion* to her son to read. Pinter worked on what is to be his finest film script between 1987 and 1990, and the film was released in 1990. Jerry Schatzberg, the American director, proposed to Pinter that he write the film script. After an initial dispute, they worked extraordinarily well together. The novella deals with the friendship between two boys in Stuttgart in 1932. In Uhlman's novella, the narrator looks back from a period of 50 years or so on his childhood memories from the relative tranquillity of New York. In the screenplay, the present is 1987 and the wealthy Manhattan lawyer Henry brilliantly played by Jason Robards (1922–2000), wrestles with a past he has vainly tried to submerge and to forget. In Pinter's transformation, unlike the novella, Henry actually travels as an old man back to the scenes of his youth to find out what actually happened to his close friend and to others. In a very moving scene, he finds the graveyard where his parents, who rather than attempt to live under the Nazis committed suicide, after they sent their son to a relative in America, are buried.

Henry or as he was known, Hans, is the son of an apparently well-respected Stuttgart doctor who was decorated with the Iron Cross for his services during the First World War. At the age of 16, at the exclusive Karl Alexander Gymnasium in Stuttgart, he forms a firm friendship with Konradin von Lohenburg. They share a passion for coin collecting, German poetry and country cycling trips. Konradin is the son of aristocrats and is invited to Henry's home but never reciprocates. The two always stop outside the gates leading up to the splendid old mansion where the young aristocrat lives. Henry sees Konradin and his parents at the opera, at a performance of *Fidelio*, Beethoven's great work expressing bravery and the desire for freedom from a brutal regime. The choice of the opera is to prove deeply ironic, given Konradin's fate. Henry is not introduced to the parents and subsequently has a prophetic nightmare. He avoids Konradin at school and then confronts him, asking 'Why cut me?' In the school gymnasium Konradin tells Henry that his mother detests Jews: even if she was dying, she wouldn't allow Henry's father, a doctor, to touch her. Konradin fights his mother for every hour he spends with what his father calls, 'little Moses'. His father tells him in words which are again in the perspective of history deeply ironic, 'The Jewish problem is bound to be resolved, sooner or later.' Konradin adds, 'He thinks it'll resolve itself' (*The Comfort of Strangers and Other Screenplays*, 1990: 85).

The film is set in 1932, just before the Nazis rise to power. It is pervaded by fear, apprehension and a growing recognition that the Nazis are not something that will disappear. The ending is both optimistic and terrible. Jason Robards as Henry/Hans (who is rarely seen without his ominous trilby hat) returns to visit a no–longer-existing school. For 50 years he hasn't spoken a word of German. Confronted by a headmaster in a new school who refuses to comment, Henry does so. Going over the wall plaque commemorating the boys at the former gymnasium who died during the Second World War, the headmaster wishes to brush aside basic facts that cannot be ignored. Pinter conveys this using an 'Umm' which is the headmaster's only reaction to Henry's questions. This attitude leads Henry to break his external reserve and tell the headmaster Brossner in no uncertain terms 'I've had no contact with Germany at all, in fact, until now. I haven't read a German book or a German newspaper. I haven't spoken a word of the German language . . . in all that time' (98).

Pinter uses a double time frame by bringing the aging Henry back to Germany to face his past and to discover what has happened to his friend. Scenes from the past, of the Nazis, of the election triumph of 31 July 1932, of Stuttgart and Germany of this period, including a seemingly peaceful countryside, are juxtaposed with those of the present, 1987. The screenplay is as much about the present as the past. As Pinter said in an interview with Michel Ciment published in *Film Comment*: 'What is left of the Nazi past is tangible in some respects, shadowy in others, possible in yet other respects, or simply non-existent among some of the young.' He adds, 'On the whole, I don't think they have really managed to overthrow the past' (21).

Pinter's additions to the novella include the depiction of Hans's father, the doctor. The return to Stuttgart and all that occurs there are the screenwriter's additions. Particularly noteworthy, apart from the visit to his parent's grave, is the visit to Konradin's former home, from which the young Hans was always shut out. It has been trans- formed into a regional government tax office where the old Henry is given a run around by an officious, polite female local government official. Another addition is his re-meeting with Konradin's cousin, Gräfin von Lohenburg, the once archetypal Aryan blond with pigtails whom it is suggested Hans lusted after. She is now a recluse, aged and embittered. She worshipped the Hitler Youth Movement and in old age pretends to be ignorant of Konradin and his fate, refusing to talk about it with Henry. For Gräfin, her youth spent under the Nazis were 'wonderful days' (94). At the conclusion of Uhlman's novel, Henry discovers that his friend Konradin was executed for partici- pating in the abortive 1944 plot to assassinate Hitler. Pinter ends the film with Brossner, the headmaster's voice over a bare 'empty execu- tion room' with 'Butcher's hooks hanging down', saying 'You don't know? He was implicated in the plot against Hitler. Executed.' This is followed by Pinter's addition: 'The butcher's hooks glint in the light from the window' (98–99). The film opens with the execution by hanging from butcher's hooks of a group of men, all participants in the plot to assassinate Hitler.

The film is full of powerful moments, dialogue and images, placing it among the most effective of all Pinter's work. Particularly remarkable is the way in which Pinter manages to convey the interplay between the present and the past. He depicts the loss of innocence of childhood friendship, betrayed personally and by tragic, brutal actual events and the way the present is shaped by the past. Among moments that stand out are Henry's encounter with a prejudiced taxi driver as he is being driven around Stuttgart to see the area and the house he grew up in. The driver's antipathy and prejudices lead to Henry's outburst against him. All Henry's bottled up anger seem to be addressed against the taxi driver, 'a man in his sixties' (95) who can remember the Nazi period, and it is cinematically, brilliantly conveyed through Jason Robards' agonised expression.

A further moving moment for many made more powerful through historical insight is when Henry's father, a proud German decorated for service in the First World War, overheard by the young Henry, disdains a Zionist who has come to visit him. The year is 1932 and the Zionist has come to warn the father who regards Hitler and Fascism as 'a temporary illness – like measles. Once the economic situation improves, Hitler will go out of fashion. He won't be necessary. Can't you see that? I know the German people. This is the land of Goethe, of Schiller, of Beethoven! They're not going to fall for that rubbish.' The unnamed Zionist leaves saying, 'You're mad.' Henry's father tells his mother 'They're such dangerous fools, these people!' (69). Shortly after, the father and mother have committed suicide, Henry their son leaves for the New World, America, and they do not witness what seems to be inconceivable, the Holocaust.

The Handmaid's Tale

Pinter's next film adaptation, Margaret Atwood's (1939–) 1986 novel *The Handmaid's Tale* has a good deal of violence, as does the adaptation based on Ian McEwen's (1948–), 1981 novel *The Comfort of Strangers*. Pinter worked on adapting Atwood's novel between 1987 and 1990. The suggestion that he work on it came from Karel Reisz. Atwood's work is set in the closing years of the twentieth century, with the vision of a dictatorial United States controlled by television evangelists and the paramilitary. Pinter's name remains on the screenplay to which he only contributed a part. He 'abandoned writing the screenplay from exhaustion' (cited Peacock, 1997: 195) and even tried unsuccessfully to have his name removed from the credits.

The Heat of the Day

The next adaptation was more successful. In 1988 Granada Television commissioned him to write an adaptation of Elizabeth Bowen's (1899–1973), novel *The Heat of the Day* first published in 1949. The setting is wartime London, the themes treachery and betrayal on a personal and national level, the masks we create in our private lives to conceal what is really happening and the fear of Fascism. This is classic Pinter terrain and is played against the background of air raids on London. Set largely in 1942, a divorced Stella Rodney (played by Patricia Hodge) finds out through Harrison (played by Michael Gambon – both he and Hodge appeared in *Betrayal*) that Robert (played by Michael York [1942–] who appeared in *Accident*), who works in a classified position in the war office, is betraying the country by passing secrets to the enemy, the Germans. Harrison, who is in Intelligence, attempts to blackmail Stella so that he can sleep with her. Stella tries to repress her knowledge that Robert is committing treason. Pinter's main transformation from the book is to emphasise Harrison's sexual obsession with Stella. At the conclusion of the novel, 15 months following Robert's death, Harrison revisits Stella. Following an air raid Harrison asks Stella, 'Would you rather I stayed till the All Clear?' (363). In the screenplay, Harrison doesn't ask, he tells Stella 'I'll stay till the All Clear.' The directions follow: '*They sit in silence. After a time, the All Clear Sounds. They do not move*' (103). The two are indissolubly linked by the events of the past: treachery has united them more than Robert's ironic idealism, his belief in the Nazi cause.

The Comfort of Strangers

Pinter's next adaptation is from Ian McEwen's *The Comfort of Strangers*. Pinter worked on the script from late 1988 to late 1989 and received a quarter of a million pounds for his work. Directed by Paul Schrader (1946–), and set in Venice, providing the opportunity for brilliant shots of the city, its architecture, landscape, canals and lagoons, the story centres on the assault upon innocence by the experienced and worldly wise. An English touring couple, Colin and Mary (performed by Rupert Everett [1959–] and Natasha Richardson [1963–]) fall prey to the older Venetian Robert (played by Christopher

Walken [1943–]) in fact a dangerous maniac and his Canadian wife
Caroline (played by Helen Mirren), his spider entrapping his prey
into his web. A central motif of the film is the relationship between
fathers and sons. At the very start of the film, the camera scans
Robert's Venetian apartment, pinpointing the clothes' brushes and
venomous razors he has inherited from his father. The first words are
Robert's as a voice-over: 'My father was a very big man. All his life he
wore a black moustache. When it turned grey he used a little brush
to keep it black, such as ladies use for their eyes. Mascara.' Other
comments follow, then a pause, and he continues: 'But he loved me.
I was his favourite' (3). The same words, excluding the comments
and those following the pause, are repeated at the end of the
film (51).

They reflect Pinter's own relationship with his father with whom
he argued fiercely. A main bone of contention may well have been
Pinter's opposition to Israel and its policies, reflected, for instance, in
Pinter's support for the campaign to release the nuclear technician
Mordecai Vanunu and Pinter's signing of petitions opposing the
Israeli government's conduct of Middle East peace talks. At times,
the fury between them must have reflected the atmosphere in
Reunion between Henry's father and the Zionist. The depth of Pinter's
love for his father is reflected in one of his finest poems, 'Death'
written just after the death of his father (*VV*: 262) and first published
in the *Times Literary Supplement* (10 October 1997: 11).

The Comfort of Strangers centres upon power and entrapment,
victims and prey. Pinter transforms parts of McEwan's novel into
ironic observations on contemporary British politics and what he
perceives to be the erosion of fundamental freedoms such as the 'freedom to be free.' At a dinner party, Robert asserts 'sometimes a few
rules – you know – they're not a bad thing.' Previously Robert speaks
of 'Lovely dear old England? . . .. Such a beautiful country. Such
beautiful traditions.' To which Mary responds, 'It's not quite so beautiful now.' Robert then goes on to express homophobia (30–31). Pinter
interjects politics into McEwen's text. In the view of Billington, *The
Comfort of Strangers* 'is not only one of Pinter's best films; it is also
one of his most acutely political. While exploiting Venice's melancholy and sinister aura, it is imbued with an irrepressible
concern for the sickness of liberty in Britain itself' (*B*: 320).

Chapter Seven
The 1990s and Beyond: Political Engagement

Pinter's operation for cancer of the oesophagus in April 2002 followed by intense chemotherapy and an autoimmune disorder called pemphigus seemed to slow him down for awhile. In October 2007 he walks falteringly with a cane, his legs are weak and he is frequently wheeled around in a chair. Yet the period from around 1990 has witnessed a flurry of activity ranging from political involvement reflected in speeches, letters, the signing of petitions, acting, to film script adaptation, directing his own work and that of others, new plays and poetry. The period 1989 through May 2005 saw him involved with five film scripts, directing the same number of plays by others and the production of seven new plays or sketches plus the writing of poetry, both personal and political.

The Trial

From 1989 to 1992, Pinter worked on adapting Franz Kafka's (1883–1924) great novel *The Trial* published in 1937. The film was released in 1993, directed by David Jones and the cast included among others, Anthony Hopkins (1937–), Jason Robards and Kyle McLaughlin in the main role as K. Pinter has been interested in the novel since he read it at school. The film adaptation had been gestating for decades and was just something he had to do. The producer was the BBC's Louis Marks (1928–) with whom Pinter previously collaborated. In his 'Producing *The Trial*: A Personal Memoir', Louis Marks recalls that Pinter suggested to him, making the film 8 years before it actually materialised. According to Marks, Pinter apparently wrote the screenplay in a 'great heat', in a short space of time, was very involved with the project and had 'Jewish affinities to Kafka'. Gale in *Sharp Cut* cites Marks as saying 'that Pinter's presence on location in Prague was quite emotional and marked by "dreamy eyes," almost as though he was in "a sort of high," especially when Vaclav Havel visited him on the set' (339).

In his 'Producing *The Trial:* A Personal Memoir', Louis Marks recalls that the film was made in what was the former Jewish quarter of Prague, the court offices used in the film were the former Gestapo Central Headquarters during the occupation of the city. The setting for the courtroom was 'an abandoned synagogue in the old Jewish quarter of Kolin, a small Bohemian town' (115), approximately an hour's drive from Prague. Pinter deliberately minimised the obviously Jewish elements in the film. He objected, for instance, to David Jones's emphasis on beards and 'Jewish' faces. Pinter observes: 'What I found absolutely natural was to tell the story straight, as it were, as a hard, taught, objective series of events.' He adds, 'The narrative is in itself remorseless and inevitable. It needs no embellishment or manipulation.' As if feeling a supernatural element at work, Pinter notes 'I have a sense of a constant and implacable force behind it, a constant and implacable presence.'

This decidedly Old Testament perspective is reinforced in Pinter's conception of Kafka's novel. For Pinter, it 'is actually about man's relation to God, and therefore if you follow the terrible tricks – the stumbles that happen in the whole work – then one has to ask what is God up to. Isn't that what the book is actually asking? What kind of game is He playing? I think that's what Kafka is asking and there is no answer' (cited Marks: 118–119). Pinter in an interview with Francis Gillen said that 'What is not in the film script is Kafka's analysis or K.'s interior monologue.' In his comments on Kafka's novel, Pinter adds that 'I felt it to be a very simple narrative. K. is arrested and everything follows quite clearly from that . . .. He neither is, nor sees himself to be, a victim. He refuses to accept that role.' Pinter also says that 'One of the captions that I would put on *The Trial* is simply: 'What kind of game is God playing?' That's what Joseph K. is really asking. And the only answer he gets is a pretty brutal one' (cited *The Pinter Review*, [1992–1993]: 62).

Lolita

Pinter spent about 6 months during 1994 wrestling with a film script of Vladimir Nabokov's (1889–1977), great novel *Lolita* (1955). Pinter was approached early in 1994 by the director Adrian Lyne (1941–), who previously had worked with Pinter in 1967, with the idea of working on a new version of Nabokov's classic novel. Pinter's version was not made, nor was David Mamet's (1947–) version which was supposed to replace Pinter's. Pinter eventually got paid for his pains. He was unhappy with Stanley Kubrick's (1928–1999), 1962 version starring James Mason, Shelley Winters (1920-2006), Peter Sellers (1925–1980) and Sue Lyon (1946–). Pinter told Steve Gale and Christopher C. Hudgins 'we barely see them touching' (Hudgins, 2001: 123), that is Humbert and the nymphette, Lolita. For Pinter, Kubrick's Lolita 'was at least 4 years too old, which goes against the point of the story' and failed to tackle 'the sexual problem inherent in the story'. Pinter also was concerned with 'the question of how far you use first-person narrative which, in principle, I'm against, but which in Nabokov is so brilliant' (cited *B*: 358).

As Hudgins indicates in his excellent account, 'Harold Pinter's *Lolita*: "My Sin, My Soul,"' it is in the 'dramatic scenes . . . where the strength of Pinter's adaptation lies'. In Pinter's version, the story is viewed through the lens of Humbert's own self-hatred. He is very much the victim of his own obsession with the nymphete Lolita that destroys him and leads him to commit murder. At the very start of the film, Humbert's car is viewed as it slowly moves down the street in 'Coalmont, Illinois 1952'. Using a voice-over, Humbert castigates himself. 'Don't come any further with me if you believe in moral values. I'm a criminal. I am diseased. I am a monster. I am beyond redemption.' He then opens the glove compartment of the car and places the pistol there in his pocket (unpublished script, BL Pinter Archive: 1). Pinter consequently 'emphasizes Humbert's depravity and ironically implicates the audience in that depravity'. Further, Humbert's sense of being beyond redemption 'Both reflects his feeling at this moment and ironically foreshadows a recognition of his own moral growth at the' conclusion of Pinter's version that yet 'still echoes the wonderful ambiguity of Nabokov's unreliable narrator'.

Pinter's script omits Humbert's time spent in a mental asylum, and also, for instance, details of his early period of his marriage to Valeria. To add to the enigmatic quality of the film script, Pinter omits the fact that Humbert employs a private detective to find out where Lolita is. Humbert's affair with Rita lasting for 2 years is among other details omitted. Hudgins notes that Pinter's 'skill in the discovery of visual or dialogic equivalents is particularly evident in his sex scenes'. These are ambiguous, suggesting Humbert's amorality, the desire to have power over another and 'Lolita's complicity as a willing, even manipulative lover' (Hudgins: 126, 129–130, 133).

The Remains of the Day

Lolita is by no means an isolated instance of Pinter's film scripts that were not shot. In the early 1990s, to take another instance, he worked on the adaptation of Kazuo Ishiguro's (1954–) fine novel *The Remains of the Day* published in 1989. Early in 1993, Pinter removed his name from the film script saying, 'it's not my script' (cited *Sharp Cut*: 366). Pinter had been fascinated by Ishiguro's narrative use of memory and the ways in which time operates on memory. However, Ruth Prawer Jhabvala (1927–) wrote a fresh screenplay on behalf of Merchant–Ivory Productions for whom she worked and who had acquired the script. The film version received various Academy nominations and was a considerable success. Pinter comments, 'There are still seven or eight scenes in the finished film that I wrote.'

'The Dreaming Child'

Another adaptation that Pinter worked on but wasn't made was from a short story by the Danish writer Isak Dinesen (Karen Blixen-Finecke [1885–1962]) called 'The Dreaming Child'. This first appeared in her *Winter's Tales* published in 1942. Pinter completed the screenplay in June 1997. Julia Ormond (1965–), the actress, producer and director bought the rights to Dinesen's story and approached Pinter who respected her work. However, Ormond, according to Pinter, 'was intent on directing, as well as producing the film and in the end it was this that brought the project to its knees. The money-men simply wouldn't give her the chance' (cited *B*: 324, 398). Dinesen's tale set in Copenhagen focuses upon Jens, an orphan child of the slums adopted by a wealthy, childless couple, Jakob and Emilie. Jens apparently quickly adjusts to his new opulent surroundings, but is unable to forget the slums. Following his death, Emilie sinks into a depression and during a countryside walk, reveals to Jakob that Jens apparently was her child. At the age of 18, she had fallen in love with Charlie Dreyer, a naval officer: whether she actually spent a passionate night with Charlie is unclear. In her fantasy, in her dreams, she seems to think she did. He died and within 2 years she married Jakob, a relative and enters into a loveless marriage, but comfortable life. She suppresses her passions and her emotions. Jens's death triggers her dreams and the wish to find expression and allows her to enter into her own inner world and beyond.

Pinter moves Dinesen's tale to Victorian England. His film script opens with a juxtaposition of Victorian poverty, wealth and repression. Francis Gillen in a fine analysis of Pinter's script, perceptively explains: 'The sordid birth of Jens', called Jack in Pinter's version, and the death of his mother, 'is interposed with scenes of Emilie's (Emily's)' in the film script 'rejection of Charlie (Charley)'. Moreover, 'light and brilliant sunlight or moonlight cuts to death and darkness, slumhouse to mansion, garden or a grand ball. Similarly, the wedding of Tom (Jakob) and Emily is interspersed with swift cuts of Charley's funeral. At the wedding, Emily's face' is expressionless. There is little dialogue in the original story, providing Pinter with an additional opportunity to create dialogue expressing internal dreams, visions and external social class differences. Pinter's emphasis is social, revealing two worlds: one of affluence; another of acute suffering. His additions 'emphasize the social themes of repression and lack of empathy'. His ending is less definite than Dinesen's. Jens/Jack the orphan boy transposed into a new world 'who died without knowing where he belonged, is the offspring of [Emily's (Emilie's)] repression and schizophrenia as well as that of her society.' Akin to Rebecca in *Ashes to Ashes*, Emily 'has begun to make connections – between her past and her present, her self and "other"' so that she has transposed into another who died giving birth in the slums to Jens/Jack (151, 153, 157).

King Lear

Tragedy, too, is the keynote of Pinter's subsequent cinematic adaptation, again not filmed, of Shakespeare's *The Tragedy of King Lear*. Pinter completed his script on 31 March 2000 after working on it for around 2 years. Pinter's memories of the play go back to his adolescence. One of his first visits to the theatre was to see Sir Donald Wolfit as Lear, and he went back to see this five times. While in rep. he played the part of one of the king's knights in Wolfit's production. For the screenplay, Pinter worked closely with the actor and director Tim Roth (1961–). In an interview with the *Independent on Sunday* published on 6 February 2000, Roth said 'This is a very hefty piece, to say the least, and I'm not interested in a bunch of people standing around a castle talking . . .. What Harold Pinter will do is to rearrange, cut and then turn it from a stage piece into cinema' (10).

Pinter does not alter Shakespeare's words or introduce his own and he deconstructs the subplot. For instance, Edgar's lengthy speech in which he decides to transform into Poor Tom is cut. Instead, Edgar stares into a stagnant pond, dirties himself and comments, 'Edgar, I nothing am.' Pinter also introduced non-dialogue scenes. Lear rides out into the storm and deserts his knights who stay outside the castle, freezing. The play is shortened considerably by dialogue cuts and cinematic adaptation allows for visual action and scenery. For instance, the film script starts with Pinter's depiction of Lear at the head of his troops following a battle in the year 1100. The following scene has no dialogue and occurs a decade later. There are shots of the outside and inside of a Norman castle, of Lear and each of his daughters and then Shakespeare's drama begins (unpublished script, BL Pinter Archive).

Sleuth

Pinter clearly enjoys adapting for the cinema. Between 2003 and May 2005 and during his life-threatening illness, he worked on rewriting for the cinema Anthony Shaffer's play *Sleuth* (1970) as opposed to the 1972 screenplay. The latter starred Sir Laurence Olivier (1907–1989) as Andrew Wyke, a well-known author of detective fiction who indulges in games of humiliation with Milo Tindle (Michael Caine [1933–]), his wife's lover. Power shifts continually in the drama until its very end. Pinter transforms Shaffer's play into one dealing with the struggle for power, possession, deception and sexual desire. At the heart of the text is the idea of two men, one young and one considerably older, entrapped in a psychological battle of wills triggered by a fight for the possession of a woman. Menace continually lurks beneath the surface of Pinter's script which is replete with cryptic language, pauses and sexual suggestiveness.

The idea of Pinter's rewriting *Sleuth* came from Jude Law (1972–), who is one of its producers and plays the role of Milo while Michael Caine now plays the older Andrew, the writer. The comedy of the earlier Shaffer version is gone. Caine's Wyke is a cockney given to sudden, violent mood shifts. According to Law, the script has a political dimension. It 'hints at [Pinter's] opinion of war . . .. Man's primal instinct is to fight, and sometimes we lose sight of what we're fighting over.' For Pinter, the conflict reflects the society in which they live which 'encourage[s] people to be highly competitive and totally selfish and uncaring of others. It's escalated, and there's a basic indifference to human fate on the part of authoritarian systems, which I believe exists not in a far away country necessarily, but here and now in this country' (cited Sarah Lyall, *New York Times*, 'Arts and Leisure', October 7, 2007: 16).

Sleuth, released in Britain and the USA in the Autumn of 2007, received largely negative reviews. It was regarded as a parody of Shaffer and Pinter's own work. Pinter's version omits 'complication and inserts surveillance cameras in and around Andrew's manse, which adds screens within screens (some in green-hued night vision) though nothing of actual thematic interest'. The dialogue is 'self-consciously synthetic'. Further, 'the story's tiresome sexual dynamics . . . suggest a link between sadism and homosexual desire. Here a brandished gun comes loaded with symbolic import, not just bullets' (Manohla Darges, *New York Times*, October 12, 2007: B14).

Oleanna

In addition to directing his own work, Pinter during the 1990s and subsequently directed the work of others. His choice of what to take on is interesting. In June 1993 he directed at the Royal Court Theatre David Mamet's play about political correctness, *Oleanna*. Pinter wrote to Mamet on 26 April 1993: 'There can be no tougher or more unflinching play than *Oleanna*. The original ending is, brilliantly, "the last twist of the knife." She gets up from the floor ("Don't worry me. I'm alright.") and goes straight for the throat. The last line seems to me the perfect summation of the play. It's dramatic ice' (cited Pinter website www.haroldpinter.org). Pinter's direction brilliantly conveys the pathos and tragic elements of the situation.

Taking Sides

In the summer of 1995, Pinter played the lead role in his own *The Hothouse* and directed Ronald Harwood's (1934–), *Taking Sides* (1995). Pinter and Harwood in 1953 both played in Donald Wolfit's company and subsequently worked together for PEN for the cause of imprisoned authors. Socially they were on good terms and even played tennis together. *Taking Sides* deals with the situation of the artist, in this instance a great conductor Wilhelm Furtwängler (1886–1954), who stayed in Germany throughout the Nazi period. The drama focuses also on the question of whether or not art, in this case music, can ever rise above political considerations. Pinter's direction allows the participants to speak for themselves. There are no clear cut answers or simple solutions given to a real dilemma.

Other Plays Directed

In a similar manner, Pinter's direction at the Bristol Old Vic in March 1996 of Reginald Rose's (1920–2002) *Twelve Angry Men* [1954], focuses on the operation of the jury system and the workings of justice. Again, Pinter is preoccupied with fundamental political concerns. He also during this period directed eight plays by Simon Gray, *Life Support* in 1997 being the seventh and Gray's *The Late Middle Class* being the eighth in 1999. Following Pinter's illness in 2004, he directed Gray's *The Old Masters*, starring Edward

Fox and Peter Bowles (1936–). Gray's play draws upon the figure of the wealthy art dealer Bernard Berenson (1865–1959) in order to explore the question of the relationship between aesthetic and spiritual values of a work of art and its material value. This naturally provided Pinter with the opportunity to direct some of his favourite themes: deception, intrigue, trust, betrayal, love and desire. These are enacted against a backdrop of the rise to power of Mussolini. The setting is a villa outside Florence owned by Berenson who lives with an ageing wife and a devoted younger secretary thus allowing for Pinteresque sexual suggestiveness.

Plays

In addition to frequent revivals of his own drama, held, for instance, at various Pinter festivals, the 1990s were a very fertile period for Pinter's own new dramatic creations. These culminated in *Celebration*, apparently his final play, performed in a double bill with *The Room*, Pinter's first play, at the Almeida Theatre on the South Bank in March 2000. July 1991 saw the first performance of the brief, approximately 10-minute running time of *The New World Order*, directed by Pinter at the Royal Court Theatre Upstairs. The end of October 1991 witnessed the premier, also directed by Pinter, of *Party Time* at the Almeida Theatre. At the same venue, *Moonlight* was performed in September 1993 before being transferred in November 1993 to the Comedy Theatre. Then in September 1996, directed by Pinter, *Ashes to Ashes*, regarded by discerning voices, as among Pinter's most moving, profound works, was premiered at the Royal Court Theatre. It was revived to much acclaim with *Mountain Language* at the Royal Court and at the New York Lincoln Center Pinter Festival in June 2001. In November 2000 the theatrical version of Pinter's un-filmed 1972 film script of *Remembrance of Things Past* was performed at the Cottesloe Theatre on the South Bank. There are in addition 'Sketches' including a female monologue, 'Tess', written in 2000 for the *Tatler* magazine and 2 years later *Press Conference*: both of which have received theatrical performances.

The New World Order

The brief *The New World Order* is an overtly political play or sketch. Lionel and Des talk prior to torturing a blindfolded man. They don't actually physically torture their victim during the sketch, merely turn to him 'in the chair', they 'walk round the chair', and at the end of the sketch 'Des shakes Lionel's hand. He then gestures to the man in the chair with his thumb.' Lionel and Des spar verbally with each other before the victim. Pinter deliberately has cut actual physical violence from the published and performed script. In the drafts found at the Pinter archive at the British Library (BL), one of the characters actually kicks the victim to the floor: Pinter has cancelled this. Language acts instead as a surrogate for physical violence and is a compound of the foul, the obscene, the political, and at times an academic, philosophical discourse. Des tells Lionel 'You called him', the blindfolded, unnamed man, 'a cunt last time. Now you call him a prick. How many times do I have to tell you? You've got to learn to define your terms and stick to them.' Des adds, 'You can't call him a cunt in one breath and a prick in the next' – the apparent logic is comic in its absurdity. As Des points out, 'The terms are mutually contradictory. You'd lose face in any linguistic discussion group, take my tip.'

Underlying the Laurel and Hardy type slapstick humour, with its delightful play on basic gender transference, there is the underlying implication here that the victim may shortly, literally lose his face! There is no triumphal boast of power, or overt sadism. In this instance, the victim has lost the power of speech and humanity, is in a catatonic state. At least Stanley in *The Birthday Party* at times attempts to answer back to his interrogators. In *The New World Order*, the victim has been silenced, even lacks a specific identity. According to Des, ironically subsequently his victim might even thank them for what they are about to do! Des reveals that 'not too long ago – this man was a man of conviction, wasn't he, a man of principle. Now he's just a prick.' To which Lionel responds, 'Or a cunt' which is humorous if it wasn't so sad. Lionel's motives, Des tells him are couched in language used by Western democracies to justify, for instance, the Gulf Wars of the 1990s and other overseas incursions: they are 'keeping the world clean for democracy' (56–58, 60).

Party Time

Party Time runs for approximately 40 minutes. Its location is not specified, but its perspective seems to be that of Pinter's London serving as a mirror for other cities and places, where affluent elites in order to maintain their own positions, squash dissent. Gavin, a wealthy suave powerful government official, 'a man in his fifties', is throwing a party at his flat situated in a very fashionable area of a city (London). Outside a violent protest is being brutally suppressed under his instructions. The 'sound of a distant helicopter' occasionally disturbs the chatter of his guests. They drink, talk about many subjects including class, games of tennis, swimming, girls and inevitably, memories. Melissa 'a woman of seventy' ([xiv]: 1) asks 'What on earth's going on out there?' and reveals that 'The town's dead. There's nobody on the streets, there's not a soul in sight, apart from some . . . soldiers' and road blocks (6–7). Melissa in the Almeida Theatre productions was brilliantly and movingly depicted by Dorothy Tutin who previously had played Kate in *Old Times* and the mother in *Mountain Language*. The conversation with the emergence of new characters, Liz and Charlotte, both of whom are in their thirties, moves from their sexual fantasies to memories of rape.

Divided into 19 separate short scenes or sequences, the brief usually no more than two or three short sentence dialogues, are frequently divided on gender lines. Liz and Charlotte's memories are followed by Fred, in his forties and Douglas, 'a man of fifty' ([xiv]) talking about the present, the 'country' (13) and their current actions. They are then followed by Emily who is in her thirties and Suki, 'a woman in her twenties' ([xiv]) who talk about 'Horse Trials' and their children (15–16). Such juxtapositions between the activities of the highly privileged, and a progress report of the actions of those protecting them, continue until the outside world, the external, intrudes. One of the guests, Dusty, who is 'in her twenties' ([xiv]) asks, 'Does anyone know what's happened to my brother Jimmy?' (22). This leads to a longer than usual speech from Terry, 'a man of forty' ([xiv]), to the effect 'that we don't discuss this question of what has happened to Jimmy, that it's not up for discussion, that it's not on anyone's agenda' (22).

The outside world intrudes. Scene 9 consists of a stage direction 'The front door is ajar. The light through it gradually intensifies. It burns into the room.' This is followed by 'Silhouetted figures moving in foreground' (24). The conversations are now longer and turn serious. For instance, Liz, who is in her thirties and married to Douglas in a lament asks 'Oh, God I don't know, elegance, style, grace, taste, don't these words, concepts, mean anything any more?' (26). Images of death, of fear, of oppression intrude among memories of an apparently peaceful past. Many things seem to have disappeared. Terry informs the guests, 'You won't find voices raised in our club. People don't do vulgar and sordid and offensive things. And if they do, we kick them in the balls and chuck them down the stairs with no trouble at all' (41). In the final scene, 19, the young angry Jimmy, the dissident, young brother appears. *Party Time* concludes with his soliloquy which, in poetic prose, expresses the way dissent has been suppressed without mercy in this apparent democracy. His name has disappeared, 'terrible noises come', he seems to be both blind and deaf. He asks himself, 'What am I?' At other times he hears 'voices, then it stops'. Jimmy's individuality has been replaced by the impersonal pronoun 'It' that takes over at the end of *Party Time* as it seems to in *monologue*. In the final two paragraphs/verses of *Party Time*, 'It' and the variant 'It's' occur 12 times. This pronoun is the final word of the play replacing the defeated, the personal 'I' found only in seven occurrences in Jimmy's speech (47).

Party Time had a largely negative reception, although its reading performance held to honour Pinter's sixtieth birthday, at the Pinter Symposium at Ohio State University, Columbus, Ohio on 19–21 April 1991, was enthusiastically received. Charles Grimes in his account of the play in his *Harold Pinter's Politics* correctly indicates the gender based aspects: 'The play identifies power with men [defined as would-be protectors] and powerlessness with women [in need of protection]' (103–104). Michael Billington writes with passion on *Party Time* to the effect that 'What was depressing was how few critics' in their hostility to the play 'stopped to ask whether there might be some truth in Pinter's central point that bourgeois privilege increasingly coexists with greater investment of power in the state and that our lives are more and more governed by a narcissistic materialism in which it is uncool to get het up about injustice and corruption' (*B*: 330).

Moonlight

Moonlight continues Pinter's obsession with memory, its unreliability, the family as a battleground, the impossibility of a return to the past, the awareness that one cannot truly know someone else, however long one has lived with them. Instead of ambiguity, however, there is an openness in the play. Its genesis lies in Pinter's reaction to the death of his mother Frances in October 1992. Around that time, Pinter was rehearsing *No Man's Land*, he was playing the role of Hirst, at the Almeida Theatre when he heard that his mother was dying. He and Lady Antonia Fraser went to Brighton to offer what comfort they could and made the funeral arrangements. Billington cites Lady Antonia as saying: 'Because of the pressure of events, Harold never had time to mourn his mother fully and *Moonlight* is, in part, an expression of that.' Moreover, she adds, that his son 'Daniel for many years never had anything to do with his grandparents.' Indeed, around this period Daniel went to live as a recluse in the Fen district, breaking off all contact with his father. Daniel had won a place at the highly select St. Paul's School and even had a poem published in a prestigious anthology of school poetry. Highly precocious, he had gained late in 1975 an award to study at Magdalen College, Oxford but following a nervous breakdown dropped out. Lady Antonia adds that *Moonlight* is 'also a play about Harold's own mortality' (*B*: 339).

Francis Gillen's very perceptive account '"Whatever Light is Left in the Dark?": Harold Pinter's *Moonlight*' (*The Pinter Review Annual Essays 1992–93*) opens with the observation that the play 'is funny, sad, moving, in some ways Harold Pinter's *King Lear*, in other's his *Tempest*'. For Gillen, *Moonlight* 'is a play about the strangeness of death and of life viewed from that perspective as the characters who peopled one man's life appear as mirror images, the presences and absences of his life' (31). *Moonlight* revolves around the dying Andy 'a man in his fifties' ([ix]) brilliantly performed by Ian Holm (1931–) who played Lenny in the first production of *The Homecoming* in

1965, Duff in the revival of *Landscape* with his then wife Penelope Wilton as Beth at the May 1994 Dublin Gate Theatre Pinter Festival and at the same venue in 2001 the role of Max in *The Homecoming*.

Rather than being split into acts and scenes, Pinter divides the play into 'three main playing areas' and sequences. In the first, Bridget 'a girl of sixteen', in what may be regarded as a prologue, exists in her own world of 'faint light'. She speaks in the present tense in positive terms of her sleeping parents whom she does not wish to awake. 'They have given so much of their life for me and for my brothers,' given 'all their love.' According to Bridget, she is 'all they have left of their life'. The play then moves into 'Andy's bedroom'. Andy, the father, 'a man in his fifties' is in bed and his wife Bel, who is fifty, sits 'doing embroidery'. The father's opening words are in the form of a question suggesting family discord and that all is not well: 'Where are the boys? Have you found them?' Hostility between husband and wife emerges. The playing area transfers to the son 'Fred's bedroom' ([ix], 1–3, 6). Fred, who is twenty-seven, is bed-ridden, Jake, the 1-year-older son is not. They reminisce in short, staccato sentences: Jake, for instance, remembers from a very early age writing poems. Both are dominated by memories of the father Andy who lies dying elsewhere. Fred and Jake's short clipped dialogue is terse, at times crude and comic. It is interrupted by the appearance of Maria who is fifty and in the past their mother's 'best friend'. She has memories of both boys as children. These memories occupy to this point the longest speech/monologue of the play. The words 'osmosis' and 'osmatic' are repeated effectively in order to convey the effect of change and of memories of the past.

The location switches back to the father's sick room, his memories of the past and belief that he 'was admired and respected' rather than 'loved' in his job as a civil servant. He kept his professional and private life separate. He tells Bel 'I kept my obscene language, for the home, where it belongs.' Bel admires Andy's present use of language when he refers to 'the paraphernalia of flowers'. However, she tells him, 'all your life in all your personal and social attachments, the language you employed was mainly coarse, crude, vacuous, puerile, obscene and brutal to a degree'. The listing, the choice of adjectives, is comic and damming. Yet is followed by redeeming qualities; Bel admits that 'this is not to say that beneath this vicious some would say demented exterior there did not exist a delicate even poetic sensibility, the sensibility of a young horse in the golden age, in the golden past of our forefathers'. On one level, she is trying to flatter, to placate her husband's anger at her, being unable to locate their absent son. On another level it suggests another side to Andy and has suggestions of a past sexual potency which has now disappeared. It is followed by 'Silence' probably affirming that Bel's remarks have some veracity.

Andy responds to his wife by reminding her of her own 'healthy lust for Maria . . ... And she for you.' This he claims didn't make him jealous either in the past or the present. This brings out, into the open, secrets. Bel reminds him that as Maria was his mistress 'Throughout the early and lovely days of our marriage' – the word 'lovely' taking on here either an ironic or a literal meaning – he had no need to be jealous. To this Andy quips that Maria 'must have reminded me of you'. A pause is followed by Andy's reflective confession 'The past is a mist' which if it wasn't so sad would be funny. In a 'faint light' Bridget, their youngest daughter, reappears. She is in her own world, 'in a dense jungle . . . surrounded by flowers'. As if he is using cinematic flashbacks, Pinter moves then to their son's bedroom where Fred and Jake act out their fantasies with names from the past and places flashing before them in their memories (15–23).

Ralph, in his early fifties, Maria's husband, appears and in a lengthy monologue, moves surrealistically and comically from soccer, 'Kissing girls. Foreign Literature. Snooker' to 'farting', 'seafaring' and 'love', although he 'preferred a fruity white wine but you couldn't actually say that in those days' (27–29). The action even moves back in time, not merely in memories and fantasies, to Jake at the age of 18, Fred at 17 and Bridget aged 14 and the relationship between them. This scene was written at Pinter's wife's suggestion. She recalls, 'We were sitting in the same room as he wrote it and Harold was reading bits out as he went along. I did just say that I'd like to know more about Bridget and her brothers so he wrote that scene in.' She adds, 'I don't really have any creative input. What I do is to provide a sounding-board' (cited *B*: 342).

The sequences then move back to the room of the dying father who laments the absence of his sons, yet remembers their negatives.

Simultaneously, he recalls in poetic language 'the twilight? The soft light falling through the kitchen window? The bell ringing for Evensong in the pub round the corner?' So, as is typical in Pinter, the lyrical is intermingled with the mundane and becomes comic owing to the unexpected juxtapositions. Andy the father then reminisces about Ralph whom he thinks, until Bel tells him otherwise, is 'probably dead' (35, 37). This leads him to Maria and his memories confessing 'I had her in our bedroom, by the way, once or twice, on our bed. I was a man at the time', and then he accuses his wife of having 'had her' too. Bel's 'I can still have you' provokes an impotent outburst from him of hostility, of regret, and claim that Bel is indulging in fantasies.

The location then moves back to 'Fred's room' (39–41) and to the brothers, then to 'Andy's room' (45), to his rambling thoughts, comic and serious on his grandchildren and his own death. The next fragment is in 'Half-light . . ... A telephone rings in Fred's room. It rings six times. A click. Silence. Blackout' as if to reinforce another facet of death. Nobody, least of all Fred, is in the room to take the phone call. The setting moves back to Andy's searching in the dark, then to his youngest daughter Bridget in a 'growing moonlight'. Bel appears, and Bridget unseen observes both her parents. Pinter transfers to 'Fred's room' (45, 48–49) with Fred still in bed and to a lengthy, comic serious banter between the two brothers focusing upon their differing reactions to their father and morality (49–62). Subsequently, back in their father's room (63–68) he and their mother reflect upon Maria, then Ralph who appears on stage, and in short, frequently one-liners, he says, 'I often think of the past' (69). They leave and Bel rings her son Jake who is with Fred 'in Fred's room' rather than as he claims at the 'Chinese laundry', to tell Jake 'Your father is very ill' (73). Both sons take turns in a comic duet to talk to their mother (73–74). In the final depiction of 'Andy's room', he is dying, still vainly waiting for his children and grandchildren to appear. His final words are for Bel to tell his daughter Bridget 'Not to be frightened', recognising his daughter's vulnerability.

In the penultimate scene, which takes place in 'Fred's room', Fred is at last 'out of bed' (76–77) and dressed in comic shorts, walking with his brother around the room again indulging in ridiculous quips and catalogues of names in an attempt to ward off reality. In his final

words, Fred confesses 'I loved him. I loved him like a father.'
Paradoxically in death, Andy the father, has gained what he craved as
he lay dying, love. The play concludes with a moving speech from
Bridget. She lives in the past, at the age of 14, when apparently she
was 'invited to a party' with her parents but arrives at a deserted
house, 'bathed in moonlight'. She is totally alone: 'I stood there in
the moonlight and waited for the moon to go down' (79–80). David
Leveaux (1958–), the director of the Almeida initial run of
Moonlight, comments that this speech 'is partly about Bridget's total
separation from her parents, her sense of exile'. He also thinks that 'it
describes the moment of her death . . . it's a speech about dying
alone' (cited *B*: 344). Bridget's words are of course open to other
perspectives: her death is not overtly indicated in the text.

   Moonlight is a poetic play about among other things death and
dying, memories, families, fathers and sons, loneliness, desire. Much
of its powerful impact depends upon the interplay of humour and
seriousness, light and dark, the past and the present depicted through
scenic and locational juxtapositions, in addition to its language
and silences. The image of moonlight is most suggestive. In the
final words of the play, Bridget 'waited for the moon to go down'
(80). Does this suggest 'that at the end of all our wandering and
intention there is only darkness after all? And is the darkness healing
as it was for her? Or only final emptiness? Or is this half light, this
moonlight, finally, existentially, our human destiny?' (Gillen: 37). In
the words of Martin Esslin, the play 'presents a deeply tragic view of
the human condition'. It 'ultimately appears as a sardonic, anguished,
and intensely felt imagistic poem about the approach of old age
and dying.'

Ashes to Ashes

Ashes to Ashes too provokes existential questions and issues. For
Esslin, it 'returns to earlier, if ambivalent modes, of Pinter's work'
that 'without exposition or closure leaves the decision as to what kind
of event is being witnessed – reality, allegory, dream, nightmare –
entirely to the spectator' (*The Pinter Review 1999 and 2000*, 2000:
26). The play was written in late January 1996 following Pinter's

return from a winter break in Barbados with Antonia. On holiday, Pinter read Gitta Sereny's (1931–) biography of Albert Speer (1905– 1981), Hitler's Minister for Armaments and Munitions. Pinter found Sereny's book published in 1995, 'staggering . . . I was very struck by the fact that Speer organised and was responsible for the slave-labour factories in Nazi Germany. Yet he was also, in some ways, a very civilised man and was horrified by what he saw when he visited the factories. That image stayed with me.'

Ashes to Ashes is pervaded with the sense that we are all capable of acts of beauty, humanity and brutality, of savagery. The contradictory nature of humanity runs through the play. There are other images that remain with Pinter from his reading occurring in the drama. The 'factories had no proper lavatories and . . . there were these primitive privies on the factor floor that were, literally, full of shit.' Pinter admits to having 'always been haunted by the image of the Nazis picking up babies on bayoneted-spikes and throwing them out of windows' (cited *B*: 374–375). Back in London in less than a fortnight, the play 'had gone through four drafts, was finished, typed up and sent on its way in the world' (*B*: 374).

There are two characters in the play, 'Both in their forties', the 'Time: Now.' The setting is 'A house in the country', with a 'Ground floor room. A large window. Garden beyond.' The place although unspecified, is England because of references to Wembley and Dorset. It is 'Early evening' and the season 'Summer'. In terms of lighting, 'The room darkens during the course of the play' and 'The lamplight intensifies'. Pinter's performance details add 'By the end of the play the room and the garden beyond are only dimly defined. The lamplight has become very bright but does not illumine the room' ([vii]: 1).

Pinter directed the premiere performance insisting that every movement and gesture has meaning. The two characters are named Devlin, a man, and Rebecca, a woman. The choice of names is not, as Billington has asserted, 'neutral' (382). Devlin has Irish and Gaelic roots meaning 'misfortune', 'fierce' and 'courage': so there are contradictions as there are in the character himself. Rebecca, or 'Rivka' in Hebrew, appears in *Genesis* as the wife of Abraham's son Isaac. She is associated with a maiden of beauty and kindness, as a symbol of loyalty to her people, and as the mother of Esau and Jacob.

Again, inherent in her name are contradictions, archetypes of fundamental human conflict, of brother against brother, of jealousy, trickery and betrayal.

In the play, Devlin stands and Rebecca sits, as if in submission. It opens with Rebecca remembering a sado-erotic ritual in which she participated without resistance with her lover. She is continually questioned by Devlin, as if being interrogated. Devlin wishes to know more and more, yet again questions whether Rebecca's lover 'ever called you darling'. He is obsessed with words and linguistic meanings. Rebecca asserts her independence from him: 'I don't want to be your darling. It's the last thing I want to be. I'm nobody's darling.' This Devlin tells her is 'a song . . . "I'm nobody's baby now."' She replies, 'It's "*You're* nobody's baby now."' The differences between 'I'm' and 'You're' (15, 17) are startling: the emphasis on the singular emphasising Rebecca's essential isolation.

The image of 'baby' and 'babies' reverberates throughout the play. Rebecca in her dreams and confusion remembers that her former lover 'a guide . . . used to go to the local railway station and walk down the platform and tear all the babies from the arms of their screaming mothers' (27). This episode reoccurs to her as she claims that she 'watched him walk down the platform' and perform the horrible act (53). Subsequently, Rebecca tells Devlin that she 'was standing in a room at the top of a very tall building in the middle of town' when she 'looked down . . . saw an old man and a little boy walking down the street. They were both dragging suitcases.' She then 'suddenly saw a woman following them carrying a baby in her arms.' They 'turned the corner and were gone' (71). The baby was a girl and the 'She' of the mother then becomes the 'I' of Rebecca.

This transference provokes Devlin into attempting the sado-masochistic ritual Rebecca's lover enacted. This time she resists, refusing his commands by not responding to his touches. Her first words are 'They took us to the trains.' This is followed not by Devlin but by an 'Echo' of her last words 'the trains'. Rebecca is now in her own world with the 'Echo' telling of how 'They were taking the babies away.' She tried to protect and save her baby but it 'cried out' (75, 77, 79), and she had to give up the baby which has become 'the bundle'. Meeting a woman she knew who asks about the baby, Rebecca denies its existence, 'I don't have a baby.' Her last words and the final words of the play are, 'I don't know of any baby' followed by a 'Long silence' and a 'Blackout'. Devlin, her tormentor, in her mind has disappeared to be replaced by her 'Echo' and is standing powerless on stage (81, 83, 85).

Ashes to Ashes is pervaded by images of brutality and savagery. It is haunted by terrible memories of genocide, of deportation, of a masochistic-erotic past relationship recalled tenderly, of the killing of innocents, of resistance. Devlin is both therapist and bully who stimulates Rebecca's memories, attempts to use them to his advantage and tries to dismiss or brush them aside. He is both a tormentor, yet is himself tormented, and unable to comprehend Rebecca.

This powerful play has evoked some of the finest critical responses to Pinter. These are to be found, for instance, in the reactions of Alastair Macaulay (1956–), the eminent chief theatre critic of the *Financial Times* and chief dance critic of the *Times Literary Supplement* and the *New York Times*. Macaulay writing in *The Financial Times* on 27 June 2001, responding to the Royal Court Theatre revival of *Ashes to Ashes*, comments, '[W]hether or not Rebecca's memories are false, they are true to some of the most appalling events of the 20th century.' It shouldn't be forgotten that the television screens of the 1990s and early twenty-first century were full of horrifying images of the conflict which erupted following the break-up of what had been Yugoslavia. They were immediately followed by images from Iraq and earlier horrific pictures from various massacres on the African continent. Devlin's is, Macaulay writes, a 'baffled inability to follow her imaginative involvement with scenes of horror'. For Macaulay 'the winged, elusive, uncapturable dark poetry of Rebecca's confused soul [is] probably Pinter's most extraordinary single achievement as a dramatist' (cited Pinter website).

Ashes to Ashes also brings out the best in Michael Billington's critical responses. He points out that 'Much of [the play's] power . . . stems from its command of theatrical atmosphere. The two figures. The spacious room. The garden beyond. The light outside darkening while that inside brightens. Even as you read it, you can see it clearly in front of you. But it also stirs memories of previous Pinter plays, while remaining hauntingly particular.' As in *The Homecoming*, there is the female who resists, adapts and gains strength. The use of popular song lyrics to play an important role in conveying memory, imagery and theme, occurs on a more sustained basis in *Old Times*. Memories and erotic dreams pervade, for instance, *Landscape*. Moreover, the universe of interrogation, of the use of power, of babies, of children, and their absence and torture, resonates in Pinter's overt political plays such as *One For the Road* and *Mountain Language*: 'What is most remarkable about' *Ashes to Ashes*, according to Billington, 'is its effortless ability to unite the domestic and the political, the English and the global' (*B*: 381–382).

In an illuminating interview with Mireia Aragay and Ramon Simó at the University of Barcelona on 6 December 1996, Pinter spoke about *Ashes to Ashes*. He began with the obvious: it 'is about two characters, a man and a woman, Devlin and Rebecca'. He continued, 'From my point of view, the woman is simply haunted by the world that she's been born into, by all the atrocities that have happened. In fact, they seem to have become part of her own experience, although in my view she hasn't actually experienced them herself. That's the whole point of the play.' He confesses, 'I have myself been haunted by these images for many years, and I'm sure I'm not alone in that. I was brought up in the Second World War.' Pinter then admits 'these images of horror and man's inhumanity to man were very strong in my mind as a young man. They've been with me all my life, really. You can't avoid them, because they're around you simply all the time. That is the point about *Ashes to Ashes*. I think Rebecca inhabits that.' The play is not confined to the Nazis; 'I'm not simply talking about the Nazis; I'm talking about us and our conception of our past and our history, and what it does to us in the present' (*VV*: 226, 228).

Celebration

Ashes to Ashes was followed in March 2000, Pinter's seventieth year, by the premiere of *Celebration* at the Almeida, directed by Pinter and performed in a double bill with his first play *The Room*. Such a coupling was suggested by Pinter's wife. The 'starting point wasn't a specific word or image. *Celebration*', Pinter reveals 'was simply drawn from accumulated memories and experiences'. Obviously, Pinter went to restaurants, in fact he dined out frequently, and the setting is a posh West End London restaurant. Pinter started to write the play when he was on holiday in Dorset with his family. They asked him to read aloud what he was writing 'Before I knew where I was, they were all collapsing with laughter and that triggered me. I went back to the study I had down there and wrote the whole damn thing in a few days. And it was at that point that the Waiter started to emerge as a character' (cited *B*: 403–404). The play is very funny, it has echoes of *The Room* and is at the same time very serious.

There are two separate restaurant tables. At a smaller table sit Russell and Suki. Russell is a shady investment banker, Suki a former secretary. At the first much larger table a wedding anniversary is being loudly celebrated by a group of former East Enders. The foul-mouthed Lambert is treating his wife Julie and his brother Matt married to Prue, Julie's sister, to a very expensive gourmet dinner. These characters have become nouveau riche. They enjoy piss-taking and insulting one another. The play is divided into the locations 'Table One and Table Two' until the groups join each other at the first table. At the opening, at the second table, Russell confesses his infidelity and makes suggestive innuendos prior to calling his wife a whore (13). At the other table, Julie invites Lambert, her husband, to 'go and buy a new car and drive it into a brick wall' (11). Lambert tells Matt that 'All mothers want to be fucked by their mothers', to which Matt responds, 'Or by themselves.' Prue his wife interjects, 'No, you've got it the wrong way round.' Matt retorts, 'All mothers want to be fucked by their sons' (17).

The more they drink, the greater the revelations that are revealed and the more outrageous the insults flung around. Fact, fantasy and the shockable intertwine. The diners at their separate tables join one another after Lambert recognises Suki: 'You see that girl at that table? I know her. I fucked her when she was eighteen.' To this, his wife Julie retorts in a reference to her husband's poetic fantasies concerning water, 'What, by the banks of the river?' (50). Lambert's recognition of Suki reminds us of her confession in the opening sequence of the play 'Oh that was when I was a plump young secretary . . . men simply couldn't keep their hands off me, their demands were outrageous' (9).

As revelations of the actual past or a fantasised past emerge, the restaurant manager, his female assistants and a waiter increasingly begin to 'interject' (30). The waiter eventually takes over the play.

He refers to the restaurant as 'my womb' (33). He has four monologues, in the manner of the only character in *monologue*, seemingly addressed to those he is waiting upon. In the first spoken to Russell and Suki, he conveys a peon of praise to a long list of writers, mainly poets, whom he claims his grandfather had 'more than a nodding acquaintance' with. They range from T. S. Eliot (1888–1965), whom his grandfather apparently 'knew . . . quite well', Ezra Pound (1885–1965), W. H. Auden (1907–1973), through to 'Dylan Thomas and if you go back a few years he was a bit of a drinking companion of D. H. Lawrence [1885–1930], Joseph Conrad [1857–1924]' and others. This list concludes with 'Thomas Hardy [1840–1928] in his dotage'.

The monologue then rambles into his grandfather's political promise before returning to literary concerns and to the great early twentieth century American writers such as Hemingway (1899–1961), William Faulkner (1897–1962), and John Dos Passos. Apparently the grandfather 'was never without his pocket bible and he was a dab hand at pocket billiards': the juxtaposition of the two is both very funny and true in general rather than personal terms, encapsulating some of the twin aspects of early twentieth century America – morality and gambling. This particular, lengthy interjection is addressed to a flabbergasted investment banker Russell who can only retort 'Have you been working here long?' It concludes with the waiter's quip that his grandfather 'was James Joyce's godmother' (31–32). Not only has he named the literary giants but those devoured by the young Pinter in his Hackney days. The trip down memory lane is as much the dramatist's as his dramatic creation.

The waiter's second set of reminiscences are aimed at the Mafioso types Lambert and Matt, both of whom claim to be 'strategy consultants' who 'don't carry a gun' (60). The waiter remembers 'a very well-established Irish Mafia in Hollywood'. He instances Clark Gable (1901–1960), Hedy Lamarr (1913–2000) and 'John Dillinger [1903–1934] the celebrated gangster and Gary Cooper [1901–1961] the celebrated film star'. He adds, somewhat incongruously and incorrectly, 'They were Jewish.' Inevitably, this is followed by 'Silence' and Julie's 'It makes you think, doesn't it?' (49–50).

His third 'monologue' is addressed to the diners who have now joined together and is provoked by Sonia's remark 'I think foreigners are charming.' The waiter recalls his grandfather's apparent personal knowledge of European personalities: 'He was an incredibly close friend of the Archduke [1863–1914] himself and he once had a cup of tea with Benito Mussolini [1883–1945].' The juxtapositions become more fanciful. The grandfather even is compared to Jesus Christ and the interjection finishes with a physical list, concluding with 'breasts, their balls', at which point Lambert intercedes with another comic one-liner, 'Well, Richard – what a great dinner!' (65–66). The guests leave, Lambert has paid for everything and the light fades slowly, with only the waiter remaining on stage facing the audience. He remembers his grandfather taking him 'to the edge of the cliffs and we'd look out at the sea' through a telescope. The final line of the play is 'And I'd like to make one further interjection' but the waiter is unable to (72).

Celebration, a play replete with crudity, catalogues of names, sexual innuendos, insults, ends on a note of incompletion with the memory of childhood and the sea. It echoes in many respects Pinter's other work. The sea and cliffs as memory and images of childhood are found in Pinter's poem 'The Islands of Aran Seen from the Moher Cliffs' (1951), in *A Slight Ache*, *Landscape*, *Old Times*, *Moonlight* and *Ashes to Ashes*. Pinter was evacuated to Cornwall from the bombing of London and went for lengthy walks along the cliffs. As with so much of his work, beginning dramatically with *The Room*, *Celebration* is also preoccupied with possession, power, sexual conflict and linguistic games among other things. Pinter is again fixated by memory and mutability. Esslin in his assessment of late Pinter notes that 'all three plays of the seventh decade of Pinter's life', *Moonlight*, *Ashes to Ashes* and *Celebration*, 'have this common feature: that they end in a melancholy soliloquy with Bridget's speech about the party that never happened, Rebecca's plaint about the lost baby, and the young waiter's unfinished interjection' (30).

Proust

November 2000 witnessed performances at the Cottesloe Theatre of Harold Pinter's and Di Treves (1947–) adaptation of Proust's *Remembrance of Things Past*. In the theatrical production, Marcel is present throughout until the very conclusion where the time that had disappeared reappears and gains permanence through art. According to Nicholas de Jongh's opening night review in the *Evening Standard*, 24 November 2000, 'Pinter's script proves once again how brilliant he is at showing how the games of sexual warfare are played and how the techniques of social aggression hit home with just the deadly flick of an adjective' (cited Pinter website www.haroldpinter.org).

The staging emphasises the social aspects of Proust. His work is set in France at the time of the Third Republic and the conflict between a fading aristocracy and rising bourgeoisie emerges theatrically. This is especially evident in the opening party set at Guermantes residence in 1921. The aristocrats talk about death and decay, a vicomtesse who has seen much better days, crosses the stage high on shots of cocaine. A nouveau riche bourgeoisie hostess employs dancers to supply the latest cabaret. Writing in the *Sunday Times*, John Peter astutely observes 'You are in a no-man's-land of reminiscence and recall, in flight from the past but with a gnawing need to reconstruct it. Time as a sequence keeps stopping, suspended in an interchange between past and present, just as it does in Pinter's *The Homecoming*, *Old Times* and *No Man's Land*' (3 December 2000, Reviews Section: 19).

'Tess' *and* Press Conference

Pinter's remaining theatrical work consists of sketches, including 'Tess' first published as a short story in the *Tatler* in November 2000 and *Press Conference*. Both were first performed at the Lyttleton Theatre, National Theatre as part of two sections of Pinter sketches on 8 February 2002. In spite of his cancer, Pinter played the role of the central protagonist in *Press Conference*. He is the Minister of Culture, previously the head of the secret police in a totalitarian state. He answers questions from the Press. His 'policy towards children' was to distrust them 'if they were children of subversives. We abducted them and brought them up properly. Or we killed them.' His policy to women? 'We raped the women. It was part of an educational process.' Critical dissent, he advises 'Leave it at home. Keep it under the bed. With the piss pot' ([10–11]). If this wasn't horrific and tragic, it would be funny and conveys a very bleak view of the world.

The dramatic adaptation of 'Tess' was brilliantly performed by Penelope Wilton. It is a very funny female monologue. Tess begins as an upper-class debutante person chatting about Mummy and Daddy and her growing up in the country. She then turns very serious, surrealistic and eccentric. Her family, her own life, her world is all mixed up, yet she maintains her upper-class pose or veneer. In fact Tess seems to transform into an expensive call girl. Pinter is again in his element, conveying class with language replete with sexual suggestiveness and innuendo, and very funny yet with the weasel underneath the cocktail cabinet waiting to emerge.

Chapter Eight
Conclusion: Cancer, the Nobel Prize, Mutations of Mortality, Poetry

The opening years of the twenty-first century have been momentous ones for Pinter. Late in 2002 cancer of the oesophagus was diagnosed, affecting the canal from his mouth to the stomach. Overcoming 95 per cent odds against surviving the operation, Pinter came through it. He then had to overcome the chemotherapy that left him feeling very weak. In 2005 he discovered that he 'had developed a rare skin disease called pemphigus: nothing to do with the cancer but it leaves terrible blisters and ulcers in the mouth. I was in and out of hospital.' Further, 'it was in the midst of all this, in October 2005, that the news of the Nobel Prize came through.' Moreover, while in Dublin for his seventy-fifth birthday on 10 October 2005 he 'had a bad fall . . . that left me with several stitches in my head' (cited *B*: 414).

While all this was going on, Pinter was receiving many accolades. In 2002 at Buckingham Palace he became a Companion of Honour. On 4 August 2004 he received the Wilfred Owen Award for Poetry for his anti-war poems. The same year as he was awarded the Nobel Prize, he gained the Prague Franz Kafka Prize. In March 2006 in Turin Pinter received the Europa Theatre Prize and in 2007 the French Legion d'Honneur. Pinter also found time to participate in demonstrations, debates, sign petitions and write letters opposing American and British actions in Iraq.

Apart From That

In May 2006 he wrote a sketch *Apart From That* and performed it with his wife. In it, two people exchange idle chatter on mobile phones. The humour, the wit is present as are the Pinteresque innuendos and undertones. Although his activities had slightly diminished, Pinter still found time for ten performances of Beckett's *Krapp's Last Tape* at the Royal Court Theatre Upstairs in October 2006. According to Billington's account 'As Krapp announced that he wouldn't want his earlier years back – "not with the fire in me now" – Pinter sat staring into the slowly fading light in aghast, agonised silence as a death-bell distantly tolled' (430).

Nobel Lecture

Such awards as the Nobel provided Pinter with the opportunity to pen powerful, rhetorical prose before a world wide platform. Such an instance is exemplified in his *Art Truth & Politics. The Nobel Lecture* delivered by Pinter on 7 December 2005 was widely disseminated in newspapers, on the web and published as a separate pamphlet by Pinter's main publishers for many years, Faber & Faber. Pinter opens by citing from his October 1958 letter to the editor of *The Play's the Thing*: 'There are no hard distinctions between what is real and what is unreal, nor between what is true and what is false. A thing is not necessarily either true or false; it can be both true and false.' Pinter believes that this continues to make sense for him as a writer but as 'a citizen I must ask: What is true? What is false?' He then goes on to exemplify the assertion that 'Truth in drama is forever elusive', using illustrations from the first line of *The Homecoming* 'What have you done with the scissors?' and the opening word of *Old Times* – 'Dark'. Pinter shows the ambiguities of both in a sequence of short paragraphs before moving to 'Political Theatre [which] presents an entirely different set of problems.' He stresses the need not to sermonise and to remain objective, instancing *Mountain Language* which 'remains brutal, short and ugly'. Pinter says, 'One sometimes forgets that torturers become easily bored. They need a bit of a laugh to keep their spirits up' and provides 'the events of Abu Ghraib in Baghdad' as an instance of this. Pinter then goes into an analysis of 'United States foreign policy since the end of the Second World War'.

Pinter moves from the example of Iraq to Nicaragua and an account of a meeting he attended at the United States' London Embassy in the late 1980s. Most of the lecture is taken up with his perspective on American foreign actions that he is opposed to. He personally attacks American Presidents and the then British Prime Minister Tony Blair. Pinter cites from a Pablo Neruda (1904–1973) poem with its 'powerful visceral description of the bombing of civilians' in this instance during the Spanish Civil War. The Nobel lecture concludes with Pinter's poem 'Death'. Pinter omits to say that the powerful poem is a response to the death of his own father in 1997. He returns to where he began, and to the 1958 letter, by asserting 'to define the *real* truth of our lives and our societies is a crucial obligation which devolves upon us all'. Pinter asserts that this 'is in fact mandatory'. His final words are that if this 'is not embodied in our political vision we have no hope of restoring what is so nearly lost to us – the dignity of man' (5, 6, 8, 10, 20, 24).

In seemingly deceptively simple prose, Pinter uses the award of the Nobel Prize to make a political statement. Morris Wernick, who has known Pinter since their Hackney childhood, wrote to his old friend that in the 'speech, there was more going on, more besides US foreign policy. I felt this particularly when you included your poem, Death, at the end of the speech. I felt, and this is hard to articulate, that it was a "sign off"' (cited *B*: 427). Pinter's Nobel speech is indeed pervaded by images of death and destruction.

Poetry

Initially screened on BBC 4 in October 2002, in April 2003 at the Tricycle Theatre, Kilburn, an adaptation of Pinter's biographical novel *The Dwarfs*, was presented in a theatrical adaptation by the film, theatre and television producer and director Kerry Lee Crabbe. Hanging outside the theatre box office was a four line poem by Pinter. It had first appeared in the *Spectator*, 15 April 2003: 13 and was subsequently included in *War* (2003), a collection of eight poems and Pinter's 'Turin Speech' given on the occasion of the award of an Honorary Degree on 27 November 2002. The poem is dated March 2003 and entitled 'Democracy'. The poems and speech found in *War* contain a hysterical quality full of imagery of death, destruction and anti-American sentiments. The collection includes the poem 'Death' but excludes the circumstances of its composition. 'Democracy' is a poem consisting of four separate sentences and rather crude. It is representative of a good deal, although not all of Pinter's poetry at this period, notable exceptions being 'Death' and 'Cancer Cells'.

An examination of Pinter's poetry is a way of summing up Pinter's concerns, his career, thematic preoccupations and conveying his genius. According to Antonia Fraser in her 'Foreword' to *Poems by Harold Pinter* chosen by her published in 2002, 'Poetry remains central to' Pinter's life. Antonia Fraser relates how at a 'dinner in a local restaurant, Harold suggested . . . that death might be necessary, otherwise the planet would be fatally over-loaded.' She 'responded with a sort of-haiku written on a napkin' celebrating her meeting with him, to which he responded, raising his glass in celebration, 'One for you, one for me' ([5]). His recent poetry, his poetry of the last 15 years or so, consists of a juxtaposition of poems celebrating his love for his wife, his obsession with his own mortality and poetic political polemics. There is not much humour involved.

'Requiem for 1945' dated 1999 and published in the *Sunday Times* (13 May 1999, Book Section 4) is a poem expressing political despair and bleakness. Its language is relatively restrained, compared with other recent poetic expressions of outrage. I must confess to finding parts of the poem ambiguous. I'm not sure that the 'they' in the first line reading 'It was like they always said', necessarily works, although it of course refers to the subjects of the next lines, for instance, to 'the blind', 'the dumb' and 'the left for dead'. The cumulative use in the poem of 'the' is powerful: it occurs six times in the second, third and fourth lines. Another ambiguity lies in the final word of the poem, 'desire': desire perhaps for life, perhaps for a different social order, personal dreams, unfulfiled, quenched by death. Unusually for Pinter's poetry, the poem is a single verse of eight lines in length: it certainly is powerful, conveying a feeling of intense bitterness (*VV*: 177).

'Requiem for 1945' is far more subtle than, for instance, 'American Football: A Reflection Upon the Gulf War' dated August 1991 with its obscene language and expression of forceful disgust. Somewhat ironically, the poem was first published in the West Village New York radical magazine *BOMB*. It had been rejected by the *London Review of Books*, the *Guardian*, the *Observer*, the *Independent* and the *New York Review of Books*. The poem is published in *War*. There is nothing subtle about it, although it could be perceived as a very accurate image of war, its cruelty and violence. Violence, threat, and fear, domination, power are not recent obsessions in Pinter's work. Indeed they run as *leit motif* through his output from his earliest writing.

Poetry also is a form Pinter has always been interested in and continually practiced. His first publication was a poem 'Dawn' which appeared in the *Hackney Downs School Magazine* in the Spring of 1947. Over a period of 60 years he has produced in addition to his plays, film scripts and other examples of his creative output, many poems including at least 90 published ones. Several collections are devoted to his poems. Some of these are published initially in now defunct journals such as *Poetry London* under a pseudonym such as 'Harold Pinta', some have been reprinted in collections of prose and poetry or in separate private press publication such as *Ten Early Poems* published by the Greville Press in 1992, or in various reincarnations of his *Collected Poems and Prose* (1986, 1991), published by Faber. The important point is that Pinter has said that poetry is the form he is concentrating on in his post-cancer period following *Celebration* and that he has given up playwriting. He is returning to, and continuing with, his first creative love, poetry.

In her brief 'Foreword' Antonia Fraser writes that her husband 'is fortunate, I believe, to be able to mark the turning-points in his life through poetry' ([5]). She instances the two verses of four lines each titled 'Paris' dated 1975 first published in *Bananas* in the winter 1977 issue and the longer 'Ghost' dated 1983 and first published in the *Times Literary Supplement* (4 November 1983). This has six two-line verses. The first poem celebrates Pinter and Antonia's 'first jaunt together in May that year', that is, 1975 ([5]). The first verse concludes with 'The light | Staggers in her eyes.' The second verse concludes with 'She', that is Antonia, 'dances in my life. | The white day burns' (7).

'Ghost' was written following the death, in the previous October, of Vivien Merchant with whom so much of Pinter's early work was intertwined since their performing together in Wolfit's company in 1953, their September 1956 marriage, the birth of their son in 1958 and the all too public divorce in 1981. 'Ghost' opens with an arresting image of strangulation similar to that in *Ashes to Ashes*: 'I felt soft fingers at my throat | It seemed someone was strangling me.' The opening line of the next verse continues the bitter–sweet contradictory states: 'The lips were hard as they were sweet.' The monosyllables then give way to a variant of the last line of the previous verse, 'It seemed someone was kissing me.' The 'I' of the poem (Pinter) is unable to communicate with the other which has been transformed by death into an 'Its.' The poem concludes 'Its eyes were wide and white its skin' which runs on into the final two lines: 'I did not smile I did not weep | I raised my hand and touch its cheek' (14). The sense of physical touch of a dead body is also echoed in Pinter's subsequent poetic lament to his dead father.

Another poem marking a personal turning point is his lament entitled 'Death' dated 1997 with beneath the title '(Births and Deaths Registration Act 1953)'. First published in the *Times Literary Supplement* (10 October 1997), as Antonia explains, the very powerful poem, one of Pinter's finest, was 'written just after the registration of his father's death at Hove Town Hall' ([5]). The poem contains the characteristic Pinter hallmarks: repetition, the language of interrogation, repetitive questions and powerful echoing pronoun usage. Only the opening two lines of the third verse and the last verse have run-on lines without questions. There are seven verses, the first, third, fourth have three lines. The second and fifth verses consist of interrogative questions: 'Who was the dead body?' and 'Was the dead body naked or dressed for a journey?' The sixth verse has four lines, each of which is a question. Particularly effective is the use of anaphora in the first two lines of the fourth verse followed by an epistrophe: 'By whom had it been abandoned?' The final seventh verse consists of five lines, each beginning with the words 'Did you' and the lines are run-on with the punctuation omitted, even at the end of the final line, 'Did you kiss the dead body'. The words, with the exception of 'abandoned' (17) at the end of the penultimate line, are monosyllabic. In the final verse, the form and content interweave most powerfully in what is a poem of personal lament for a dead father, not a political poem. The latter reading is probably encouraged by the inclusion of 'Death' as the final poem in *War* but without the details of the 'Births and Deaths Registration Act of 1953' omitted following the title and the 1997 date is also left out at the end ([21]).

'Cancer Cells', dated March 2002, is another poem marking 'the turning-points in' Pinter's life (Antonia Fraser, 2002: [5]). In this instance, it is Pinter's almost fatal illness. On the other hand, 'To My Wife', dated June 2004, first published in the *Guardian* in July 2004, celebrates Pinter's love for his wife. Both illustrate Pinter's use of differing verse forms. In the first, two verses of two lines extend to a third and as the 'Cancer cells', the subject of the poem, spread into a seven-line fourth verse, subsiding with treatment into the last verse of four lines. This opens 'The black cells will dry up and die'. It concludes on a note of doubt: 'You never know, they never say' (18).

'To My Wife', written after the publication of *Poems by Harold Pinter Chosen by Antonia Fraser*, is five verses of two lines each of celebration. It is republished in Pinter's *Six Poems for A* (2007). The first line of the opening two verses begins with the personal 'I'. The opening word of the remaining three verses begins with 'You'. The poem opens 'I was dead and now I live | You took my hand' and closes 'You are my life | And so I live'. In each verse of the poem, the personal pronouns most effectively intertwine. The words are largely monosyllabic with much repetition and interplay between tenses (9).

To summarise, tender lyricism found also in dramatic form such as in *Landscape*, for instance, is prevalent in the later love poems having Antonia Fraser as their subject. The violent, vicious, visceral, expletive Pinter however occurs frequently in his later poetry. See, for instance, the poems in the 2003 collection *War* with titles such as 'God Bless America', 'The Bombs', 'Democracy', 'Weather Forecast' and 'American Football'. This poetry is overtly political with its immediate context hostility to a major, the major wielder of power on the international scene. An example of such poetry is 'The Special Relationship' dated August 2004, and published in the *Guardian* (9 September 2004, G2: 4) with its ironic title referring to what was assumed to be a special relationship between two countries, the UK and the USA. The effect of the poem depends partly on its variations upon the repetitive, 'go off' found in the first five lines, lines seven and eight. The first four verses of three lines each begin with 'The'. Each word until the final two lined last verse consists of four monosyllables. The final two lines begin with a specific 'A' rather than the general 'The' in the penultimate line with 'another' being the only possibly non-monosyllabic word in the poem. This penultimate line is the longest in the poem, having seven words. The last line, with its, as some may find, disgusting sexual image – an ambivalent one – reverts to the four-word pattern for the rest of the poem, 'And sucks his lust.'

Such venom is also found in Pinter's 'Body' published in the *Saturday Guardian*, (25 November 2006: 23). This eight-line run-on single verse poem lacking punctuation is obsessed with death and the dichotomy between 'Laughter' and 'the dead'. Repetition and slight word changes are evident in, for instance, the opening two lines: 'Laughter dies out but is never dead | Laughter lies out the back of its head'. The lines rhyme respectively concluding 'dead', 'head', 'said', then the variant 'head', 'dead', 'spread'. The final two lines begin with the words 'Sucked in' and conclude with 'severed head' and 'laughing dead'. A poem beginning affirmatively with 'Laughter' has been transformed by the imagery of the grotesque. Also evident is Pinter's obsession with dead bodies and the poem is reminiscent of the tortured, paranoid visions inherent in some of his poems of the 1950s, for instance, 'The Error of Alarm' and 'Afternoon', both dating from the 1956–1957 period. This bleakness, sense of nihilism without humour, is found also in the poem 'Later' (1974) and also in some of the plays, most notably in *Mountain Language* and *Ashes to Ashes*. As Pinter told Kirsty Wark in a television interview, 'Shall I tell you what I really think?' and he continues, 'I think that life is beautiful but the world is hell' (cited Woolf, *The Guardian*, 12 July 2007: 24).

'The Mirror' and Conclusion

In his finest drama, poems, prose, film scripts and adaptations, Pinter superbly controls his emotions and feelings, shaping them through poetic techniques through repetition, slight variation through word and line length, the use of rhythm, alliteration and assonance. The traditional techniques of the poet are brought to bear to transform feeling into form. Within the dramatic context, there is a speech driven nature about Pinter's poetry. The speeches give his writing a duration, a time as well as an embodied spatial/temporal situation.

His pauses serve to emphasise the arbitrary relationship between the written text and the duration, the time a voice will give it. After all, as a dramatist, Pinter's concern for language is with speech as much as with writing, or at least the relationship between the two. Also, he hasn't lost the ability to surprise, to reinvent, or his remarkable fecundity of invention. For instance, the undated, very short single paragraph, 178-word, 24-short-sentence prose 'The Mirror' published in *Areté* 23 (Summer/Autumn 2007), [59] is in the words of Craig Raine (1944–), the eminent poet and critic and editor of *Areté*, 'a prose poem'. That is, 'a piece of prose too short to be a short story or what the Germans call *eine kleine Prosa*. It's rather terrific' (e-mail to the author: 30 October 2007).

Reminiscent of passages in *The Dwarfs* or a passage in *monologue*, it contains an interplay between the present and the past. The last sentences are revealing: 'I no longer remember her name . . . but that is all in the past . . . I've changed my face.' This preoccupation with memories, identity and verification reverberates through the piece and Pinter's work. There are London locations ranging from the posh 'St. John's Wood High Street' to the less salubrious 'Shepherd's Bush Green'. Words such as 'face' and 'eyes' are repeated, suggesting perhaps the speaker's present impotence, there are colour contrasts, between 'black' and 'blue' eyes. The 'I' who 'looked in the mirror, is unable to remember whether he is thinking of 'Lucy or Lisa'. Colloquial word usage such as 'catnap' is present in this very Pinteresque 'The Mirror' ([59]).

A major element in Pinter's artistic achievement is one of return and renewal in poetry, through drama and prose containing poetry of landscape, memory and power play, and the evocation of personal violence. The latter is transformed into a vision of international political military destruction in which many lives are lost. It also combines with a tremendous expression, heightened by cancer, of personal mortality, of mutability which evokes those great Pinteresque themes of the passing of time and memory – forever present in his work. Of course Pinter's use of variation in the poems, is itself reflecting the process of time. In a sense, his themes are recently made more cogent with forebodings of death just around the corner. Combined with this is the expression of love: 'forever alive in my heart and my head' (*Six Poems for A*, 2007: 10).

Notes

1. Billington, 2007. Henceforth referred to as *B* followed by the page reference.
2. Henceforth referred to as *VV*.
3. See Esslin (1970), *The Peopled Wound*, Chapter 4 and Steven H. Gale (1977), *butter's going up*, 270: Gale has a succinct explanation of Pinter's techniques, see for instance, his remarks on Pinter's pauses and silences (273–274).
4. See Harold Pinter, '*First Draft, The Homecoming*' and Francis Gillen, 'Pinter at Work: An Introduction to the First Draft of *The Homecoming* and Its Relationship to the Completed Drama', *The Pinter Review Collected Essays 1997 and 1998*: [1] –30, [31] –47.

Bibliography

Primary Sources

A comprehensive account of Pinter's output is found in William Baker and John C. Ross, *Harold Pinter: A Bibliographical History*. London: The British Library; New Castle, DE: Oak Knoll Press, 2005. Much of Pinter's work is available in either the Faber & Faber collected editions of Pinter or in the same publisher's *Various Voices: Prose, Poetry, Politics, 1948–2005*, London: Faber & Faber, 2005.

A. Plays and Sketches for the Stage, Radio and Television

Apart From That (2006) unpublished sketch.

Ashes to Ashes. London: Faber & Faber, 1996.

The Basement. BBC 2 TV. 1967 (British Library Pinter Archive) In *Tea Party and Other Plays*. London: Methuen, 1967.

Betrayal. London: Eyre Methuen, 1978.

The Birthday Party. London: Methuen, 1963 [first published by Encore Publishing Co. Ltd, 1959].

The Black and White (as short story, 1955) in *Sketches from One to Another*. London: Samuel French, 1960.

The Caretaker. London: Methuen, 1960 [first published Encore Publishing Co. Ltd, 1960].

Celebration (1999) in *Celebration and The Room*. London: Faber & Faber, 2000.

The Dwarfs in *A Slight Ache and Other Plays*. London: Methuen, 1961.

The Dumb Waiter (1957) in *The Birthday Party and Other Plays*. London: Methuen, 1960.

The Examination (as a short story in *Prospect* [summer of 1959]: 21–25),
also in *Ten of the Best British Short Plays*, ed., Ed Berman. London:
Inter-Action, 1979.

Family Voices: A Play for Radio With Seven Paintings by Guy Vaesen.
London: Faber & Faber, 1981.

*Five Screenplays: The Servant, The Pumpkin Eater, The Quiller Memoran-
dum, Accident, The Go-Between*. London: Methuen, 1971.

The Homecoming. London: Methuen, 1965.

The Hothouse (1958). London: Eyre Methuen, 1980.

Landscape (1967) in *Landscape* and *Silence*. London: Methuen, 1969.
Also as BBC Radio Play, April 1968.

The Lover (1962) in *The Collection* and *The Lover*. London: Methuen,
1963.

monologue. London: Covent Garden Press, 1973. Reprinted in *Plays 4*.
London: Eyre Methuen, 1981.

Moonlight. London and Boston: Faber & Faber, 1993.

Mountain Language. London and Boston: Faber & Faber, 1988.

The New World Order (1991) in *Party Time and the New World Order*.
New York: Grove Press, 1993.

No Man's Land. London: Eyre Methuen, 1975.

Night (1969) in *Landscape* and *Silence*. London: Methuen, 1969.

A Night Out (1961) in *A Slight Ache and Other Plays*. London: Methuen,
1961.

Night School (1966) in *Tea Party and Other Plays*. London: Methuen,
1967.

One for the Road. London: Methuen, 1984 [a Methuen New
Theatrescript].

Other Places: Four Plays. New York: Dramatists Play Service, Inc., 1984.

Other Places: Three Plays. London: Methuen, 1982.

Old Times. London: Methuen, 1971.

Party Time and The New World Order: Two Plays by Harold Pinter. New
York: Grove Press, 1993.

Precisely (1983) in *The Big One: An Anthology of Original Sketches, Poems,
Cartoons and Songs on the Theme of Peace*, ed. Susannah York and
Bruce Bachle, London: Methuen, 1984.

Press Conference. London: Faber & Faber, 2002.

Remembrance of Things Past, 1972 (adapted by Harold Pinter). London:
Faber & Faber, 2000. (with Di Treves).

The Room (1957) in *The Birthday Party and Other Plays*. London: Methuen, 1960.

Silence (1968) in *Landscape and Silence*. London: Methuen, 1969.

A Slight Ache (1958) in *A Slight Ache and Other Plays*. London: Methuen, 1961.

'Tess: A Short Story By Harold Pinter', *Tatler*, (November 2000): 75–76. Short story performed as a dramatic sketch.

Victoria Station (1982) in *Other Places: Three Plays*. London: Methuen, 1982.

B. Film Adaptations

Some of Pinter's screenplays may be found in the Faber edition of his *Collected Screenplays*, 3 vols. London: Faber & Faber, 2000.

The Caretaker [In US, *The Guest* (1964)] screenplay 1962–1963. Script at the British Film Institute.

Collected Screenplays. 3 vols. London: Faber & Faber, 2000.

The Comfort of Strangers and Other Screenplays. London and Boston: Faber & Faber, 1990.

'The Dreaming Child' (1997) [screenplay published but not yet filmed] in *Collected Screenplays*, Vol. 3.

The Dwarfs. Initially screened on BBC 4 in October 2002, in April 2003 at the Tricycle Theatre, Kilburn, an adaptation of Pinter's biographical novel *The Dwarfs*, by Kerry Lee Crabbe. London: Faber & Faber, 2003.

The French Lieutenant's Woman (1981) in *The French Lieutenant's Woman and Other Screenplays*. London: Methuen, 1982. Also see *Collected Screenplays* Vol. 3.

The Go-Between (1964, 1969) in *Five Screenplays*. London: Methuen, 1971. Also in *The Servant and Other Screenplays*. London and Boston: Faber & Faber, 1991 and see *Collected Screenplays* Vol. 2.

Heat of the Day. London and Boston: Faber & Faber, 1989. Also in *Collected Screenplays*, Vol. 3.

Langrishe Go Down in *The French Lieutenant's Woman and Other Plays*. London: Methuen, 1982. Also in *Collected Screenplays*, Vol. 1.

The Last Tycoon (1975) in *The French Lieutenant's Woman and Other Plays*. London: Methuen, 1982. Also in *Collected Screenplays*, Vol. 1.

Lolita (1994) [screenplay not used] in the British Library Pinter Archive.

The Proust Screenplay: À la Recherché du Temps Perdu (screenplay not filmed, 1972, published as *The Proust Screenplay.* [in collaboration with Joseph Losey and Barbara Bray]. London: Eyre Methuen, 1978).

The Pumpkin Eater (1963) in *Five Screenplays.* London: Methuen, 1971. Also in *Collected Screenplays*, Vol. 1.

The Quiller Memorandum (1966) in *Five Screenplays.* London: Methuen, 1971.

The Remains of the Day [screenplay, mainly not used, not published (1990)] British Library Pinter Archive.

Reunion (1987–1988) in *The Comfort of Strangers and Other Screenplays.* London: Faber & Faber, 1990. Also in *Collected Screenplays*, Vol. 2.

Servant in *Five Screenplays.* London: Methuen, 1971. Also in *Collected Screenplays*, Vol. 1.

Shakespeare's *The Tragedy of King Lear* [2000]. Film adaptation not made, British Library Pinter Archive.

Sleuth. (2002–2005) British Library Pinter Archive.

The Trial (1989–1992). London and Boston: Faber & Faber, 1993.

Victory (1982) [unproduced screenplay] in *The Comfort of Strangers and Other Screenplays.* London: Faber & Faber, 1990.

C. Poetry

'American Football (Reflection on the Gulf War)', *BOMB*, XXXVIII (Winter 1992): 82 and *The Pinter Review, V: Annual Essays for 1991.* (1991): 41. In *VV* and *War*.

'Body', *Saturday Guardian*, (25 November 2006): 23.

'The Bombs', *Independent*, (15 February 2003). In *VV* and *War*.

'Cancer Cells', *Guardian*, (14 March 2002), G2: 5. In *VV*.

'Chandeliers and Shadows', *Poetry London*, 5 (19 August 1950): 8–10. As Harold Pinta. In *VV*.

'Dawn', *Hackney Downs School Magazine*, 161 (Spring 1947): 27.

'Death' (Births and Deaths Registration Act, 1953) *Times Literary Supplement*, 4932 (10 October 1997): 11. In *VV* and *War*.

'Democracy', *Spectator*, (15 April 2003): 13. In *VV* and *War*.

'Episode', (1951), in *Poems*, 1968.

'God Bless America', *Guardian* (22 January 2003), G2: 4. In *VV* and *War*.

'Ghost', *Times Literary Supplement*, 4205 (4 November 1983): 1204. In *VV*.

I Know the Place. Warwick: The Greville Press, 1979.

'I Shall Tear off my Terrible Cap', *Poetry Quarterly*, 13: 2 (Summer 1951): 59. As Harold Pinta.

'The Islands of Aran Seen from the Moher Cliffs' (1951), *Poems*, 1968. In *VV*.

'Joseph Brearley 1909–1977', in *Soho Square* II (1982): 182. In *VV*.

'Kullus' (1949) in *Poems*. London: Enitharmon Press, 1968.

'New Year in the Midlands', *Poetry London*, 5 (19 August 1950): 8–10. As Harold Pinta. In *VV*.

'O Beloved Maiden', *Hackney Downs School Magazine*, 162 (Summer 1947):14.

'One a Story, Two a Death', *Poetry London* 6: 22 (Summer 1951): 22–23. As Harold Pinta.

'Paris' (1975), in *Bananas* 9 (Winter 1977): 35. In *VV*.

'Poem' (1953) in *Poems*, 1968. In *VV*.

Poems. London. Enitharmon Press, 1968.

Poems [second edn. with nine added poems]. London: Enitharmon Press, 1971.

Poems by Harold Pinter chosen by Antonia Fraser. Warwick: The Greville Press, 2002.

'Requiem for 1945' (1999), *Sunday Times* (13 May 1999, Book Section 4). In *VV*.

'School Life' (1948). In *VV*.

Six Poems for A (2007). Warwick: The Greville Press, 2007.

'The Special Relationship' (August 2004) *Guardian* (9 September 2004), G2: 4. In *VV* and *War*.

Ten Early Poems. Warwick: The Greville Press, 1992.

'To My Wife' (June 2004) *Guardian* (22 July 2004), G2: 4. In *VV*.

'A View of the Party', (1958) in *Poems*, 1968.

'Weather Forecast', *Guardian* (20 March 2003), G2: 2. In *VV* and *War*.

Various Voices: Prose, Poetry, Politics, 1948–2005. London: Faber & Faber, 2005. [*VV*]. Contains some of Pinter's poetry.

War. London: Faber & Faber, 2003. Contains also Pinter's prose.

D. Fiction

'The Black & White. An Unpublished Text by Harold Pinter'. *Flourish*, 4 (Summer 1965): 4. 'The Royal Shakespeare Club Newspaper'. Also in the *Transatlantic Review*, 21 (Summer 1966): 51–52.

The Dwarfs: A Novel. London: Faber & Faber, 1990. Adapted from the novel as a play by Kerry Lee Crabbe. London: Faber & Faber, 2003.

'The Mirror', *Areté* 23 (Summer/Autumn 2007), [59]. Prose piece.

E. All Other, Including Interviews and Editions of Collected or Selected Works

Ian Smith, compiled and edited. *Pinter in the Theatre*. London: Nick Hern Books. 2005 [hereinafter referred to as Smith, *Pinter*]; and Mark Batty. *About Pinter: The Playwright and the Work*. London: Faber & Faber, 2005 contain previously published interviews with Pinter, as does Mel Gussow. *Conversations with Harold Pinter*. London: Nick Hern Books, 1994.

Ando, Roberto, 'Ritratto di Harold Pinter', *RAI-SAT*. 1998. [Italian television interview].

'The Art of the Theatre' (interview with Lawrence Bensky) *Paris Review* no. 39 (Fall 1966): 13–37.

Arthur Wellard. London: Villiers, 1981. In *VV*.

'Blood Sports', *Hackney Downs School Magazine* no. 163 (Autumn 1947): 23–24

Cambridge University Magazine. Programme note to *The Room* and *The Dumb Waiter*. 1956. In Gussow, *Conversations*.

The Catch a Correspondence. [Introduction by Alan Wilkinson.] Charingworth: Alan Wilkinson, The Evergreen Press, 2003.

Ciment, Michel. '*Reunion*: Harold Pinter Visually Speaking'. *Film Comment*, XXV, no. 3 (May–June 1989): 20–22.

Collected Poems and Prose. London: Methuen, 1986. And London and Boston: Faber & Faber, 1991.

[Contribution to 'Jimmy']. [*Jimmy*.] *Jonathan Wax*. London: Pendragon, 1984. In *VV*.

'Filming *The Caretaker*: Harold Pinter and Clive Donner Interviewed by Kenneth Cavander', *Transatlantic Review* 13 (Summer 1963): 17–26.

'First Draft, *The Homecoming*', *The Pinter Review Collected Essays 1997 and 1998*: [1]–30.

Gussow, Mel. *Conversations with Harold Pinter*. London: Nick Hern Books, 1994.

[Harold Pinter] In Conversation at the Royal Court Theatre, 20 October 2005. British Library Sound Archives.

'In view of its progress in the last decades, the Film is more promising in its future as an art form than the Theatre'. *Hackney Downs School Magazine*, no. 164 (Spring 1948): 12.

Interview with Kenneth Tynan BBC, 19 August 1960. In Gussow, 'A Conversation (Pause) with Harold Pinter' in the *New York Times Magazine,* (5 December 1971): 53.

'James Joyce'. *Hackney Downs School Magazine*, no. 160 (Christmas 1946): 32.

'Just a simple little love story?' *Radio Times*, 16–22 September 1978, 80–83, 85 (Harold Pinter with Judi Dench and David Jones talk to Jack Emery regarding *Langrishe Go Down*).

'Letter to Peter Wood, Director of *The Birthday Party*', dated 30 March 1958. *Kenyon Review*, III, no. 3 (Summer 1981): 2–5. In *VV*.

Lyall, Sarah. 'Still Pinteresque', *New York Times*, 'Arts and Leisure', (7 October 2007): [1], 16. Contains extracts from discussion with Pinter.

Mac. [London]: Emanuel Wax for Pendragon Press, 1968. In *VV*.

'Memories of Cricket', *Daily Telegraph Magazine* (16 May 1969): 25–26.

'A Note on Shakespeare' [prose essay dated 1950] *Granta* 59 (Autumn 1993): 252–254. In *VV*.

'Orange Screen Writers Season at the British Library'. Harold Pinter interviewed by Peter Florence at the British Library (9 February 2004). British Library Sound Archives.

'Personal Wonderlands', PEN Discussion (25 November 2003). British Library Sound Archives.

[Pinter on] *The Trial*, *Pinter Review*, [1992–1993]: 61–62.

Pinter Website: www.haroldpinter.org

The Proust Screenplay, radio adaptation of (1995) National Sound Archive London.

'The Queen of All the Fairies' [1952?] unpublished autobiographical prose work, British Library, Pinter Archives.

'Radical Departures: Harold Talks to Anna Ford', *Listener*, 120, no. 3086 (27 October 1988): 5–6. In Smith, *Pinter*.

'Realism and Post-Realism in the French Cinema', *Hackney Downs School Magazine*, no. 163 (Autumn 1947): 13.

'Reply to Open Letter By Leonard Russell', *Sunday Times* (14 August 1960): 21.

Silence (August 1970) as a radio drama. British Library BBC Sound Archives.

Speech, 'Writing for the Theatre'. First published as 'Pinter: Between the Lines', *Sunday Times* (4 March 1962): 25. In *VV*.

'Trying to Pin Pinter Down: Interview with Marshall Pugh'. *Daily Mail* (7 March 1964): 8.

'Two People in a Room: Playwriting', the *New Yorker*, 43 (25 February 1967): 34–36.

University of Turin Speech (27 November 2002). In *VV*.

Various Voices: Prose, Poetry, Politics, 1948–2005, London: Faber & Faber, 2005.

War. London: Faber & Faber, 2003 [prose and poetry].

'Writing, Politics, and *Ashes to Ashes*: An Interview With Harold Pinter', with Mireia Aragay and Ramon Simó. *The Pinter Review Annual Essays 1995 and 1996* (1997): [4]–15.

Secondary Sources

A. Writings About Pinter

This listing is confined to those books and articles mentioned in this study. An excellent guide to the many studies of Pinter is found in Steven H. Gale, *Harold Pinter: An Annotated Bibliography*. Boston: G. K. Hall & Co., 1978. This needs supplementing with Steven H. Gale, *Critical Essays on Harold Pinter*, Boston: G. K. Hall & Co., 1990, Susan Hollis Merritt, *Pinter in Play: Critical Strategies and the Plays of Harold*

Pinter. Durham, NC and London: Duke University Press, 1990 and Peter Raby, ed. *The Cambridge Companion to Harold Pinter*. Cambridge: Cambridge University Press, 2001. Merritt provides an indispensable listing of primary and secondary Pinter materials in her 'Annual Bibliography' found in *The Pinter Review*, edited by Francis Gillen and Steven H. Gale. Tampa, FL: The University of Tampa Press, 1987.

1. *Books*

Baker, William and John C. Ross. *Harold Pinter: A Bibliographical History*. London: The British Library and New Castle, DE: Oak Knoll Press, 2005.

Baker William and Steven E. Tabachnick. *Harold Pinter*. Edinburgh: Oliver and Boyd, 1973.

Batty, Mark. *About Pinter: The Playwright and the Work*. London: Faber & Faber, 2005.

Billington, Michael. *Harold Pinter: New and Updated Edition*. London: Faber & Faber, 2007.

Burkman, Catherine H. *The Dramatic World of Harold Pinter*. Columbus, OH: Ohio State University Press, 1971.

Esslin, Martin. *The Peopled Wound: The Work of Harold Pinter*, 1970.

—. *Pinter: A study of his plays: third and expanded edition*. London: Eyre Methuen, 1977.

Gale, Steven. *butter's Going Up: A Critical Analysis of Harold Pinter's Work*. Durham, NC: Duke University Press, 1977.

—. *Critical Essays on Harold Pinter*. Boston: G.K. Hall & Co., 1990.

—. ed. *The Films of Harold Pinter*. Albany, New York: SUNY Press, 2001.

—. *Harold Pinter: An Annotated Bibliography*. Boston: G.K. Hall & Co., 1978.

—. *Sharp Cut: Harold Pinter's Screenplays and the Artistic Process*. Lexington, KY: University Press of Kentucky, 2003.

Gordon, Lois, ed. *Pinter at Seventy: A Casebook*. London and New York: Routledge, 2001.

Grimes, Charles. *Harold Pinter's Politics: A Silence Beyond Echo*. Cranberry, NJ: Associated University Press (Fairleigh Dickinson University Press), 2005.

Hayman, Ronald. *Contemporary Playwrights: Harold Pinter*. London: Heinemann, 1976.

Merritt, Susan Hollis. *Pinter in Play: Critical Strategies and the Plays of Harold Pinter.* Durham, NC and London: Duke University Press, 1990.

Peacock, Keith. *Harold Pinter and the New British Theatre.* Westport, CT: Greenwood, 1997.

Raby, Peter, ed. *The Cambridge Companion to Harold Pinter.* Cambridge: Cambridge University Press, 2001.

Smith, Ian, compiled and edited. *Pinter in the Theatre.* London: Nick Hern Books, 2005.

Taylor, John Russell. *Anger and After: A Guide to the New British Drama.* London: Methuen, 1962. Harmondsworth, Middlesex: Penguin Books, revised edition 1963.

2. *Articles and Reviews*

Ben-Zvi, Linda. '*Monologue*: The Play of Words', in *Pinter at Seventy: A Casebook*, ed. Lois Gordon. London: Routledge, 2001: 81–93.

Boulton, James T. 'Harold Pinter: *The Caretaker* and Other Plays', *Modern Drama* (September 1963): 131–40.

Bryden, Ronald. 'Pinter's New Pacemaker', review of *Old Times*, *The Observer* (6 June 1971): 27.

Darges, Manohla. Review of *Sleuth*, *New York Times* (October 12, 2007): B14.

De Jongh, Nicholas. Review of *Remembrance of Things Past*, *Evening Standard* (24 November 2000): cited www.haroldpinter.org.

Dickson, Wheeler Winston. 'The Eternal Summer of Joseph Losey and Harold Pinter's *Accident*', in Gale, *Films*, 2001: 27–37.

Esslin, Martin. 'Harold Pinter: From *Moonlight* to *Celebration*', *The Pinter Review 1999 and 2000*, 2000: [23] –30.

Gillen, Francis. 'Isak Dinesen with a Contemporary Social Conscience: Harold Pinter's Film Adaptation of "The Dreaming Child"', in Gale, *Films*, 2001: 147–158.

—. 'Pinter at Work: An Introduction to the First Draft of *The Homecoming* and Its Relationship to the Completed Drama', *The Pinter Review Collected Essays 1997 and 1998*: [31]–47.

—. '. . ."Whatever Light Is Left in the Dark,": Harold Pinter's *Moonlight*', *The Pinter Review Collected Essays, 1992–1993*: 31–37.

Hall, Peter. 'Directing Pinter', *Theatre Quarterly*, IV, 16 (November 1974–January 1975): 4–17.

Hobson, Harold. 'Paradise Lost', review of *Landscape* and *Silence*, *Sunday Times* (6 July 1969): 52.

—. 'The Screw Turns Again', review of *The Birthday Party*, *Sunday Times* (25 May 1958).

Hudgins, Christopher. 'Harold Pinter's *The Comfort of Strangers*: Fathers and Sons and Other Victims', *Pinter Review: Annual Essays 1995–1996* (1997): 54–72.

—. 'Harold Pinter's *Lolita*: "My Sin, My Soul"', in Gale, *Films*, 2001: 123–146.

Losey, Joseph, on *The Go-Between*, *Time* (9 August 1971): 45.

Macaulay, Alastair, on *Ashes to Ashes*, *The Financial Times* (27 June 2001): cited www.haroldpinter.org.

Marks, Louis. 'Producing *The Trial*: A Personal Memoir', in Gale, *Films*, 2001: 109–121.

Peter, John, on *Proust*, *Sunday Times* (3 December 2000, Reviews Section): 19.

'Profile: Playwright on his own', *The Observer* (15 September 1963): 13.

Roth, Tim, on *King Lear* adaptation, *Independent on Sunday* (6 February 2000): 10.

Rosselli, John. 'Between Farce and Madness', review of *The Caretaker*, *Manchester Guardian* (29 April 1960): 13.

Shulman Milton, 'Sorry, Mr. Pinter, You're Just Not Funny Enough', review of *The Birthday Party, Evening Standard* (20 May 1958): 6.

Spencer, Charles. 'Pinter's Prescient Missing Link', reviewing the National Theatre revival of *The Hothouse*, the *Daily Telegraph* (19 July 2007). www.telegraph.co.uk.

Supple, Barry, 'Pinter's Homecoming', *Jewish Chronicle* (25 June 1965): 7, 31.

Tynan, Kenneth. Review of *The Birthday Party*, *The Observer* (25 May 1958): 15.

—. 'A Verbal Wizard in the Suburbs', review *The Caretaker*, *The Observer*, (5 June 1960): 16.

Woolf, Henry. 'My Sixty Years in Harold's Gang', the *Guardian* (12 July 2007), G2: 23–25.

B. General Works

Archibald, William. *The Innocents*. New York: Coward-McCann, 1950.

Atwood, Margaret *The Handmaid's Tale*. London: Cape, 1986.

Bakewell, Joan. *The Centre of the Bed*. London: Hodder & Stoughton, 2003.

Baron, Alexander. *With Hope, Farewell*. London: Jonathan Cape,1952.

Beckett, Samuel. *Krapp's Last Tape and Embers*, Faber & Faber, 1959.

—. *Murphy*. London: Routledge, 1938.

—. *Watt* in *Poetry Ireland*, 1950.

—. *Waiting for Godot*. London: Faber & Faber, 1956.

Besant, Walter. *The Eulogies of Richard Jefferies*. London: Chatto & Windus, second edition, 1889.

Brecht, Bertolt. *The Mother* (1930–1931) *Die Mutter, Versuche*, Heft 7 (1933). London: Methuen, 1978.

Bowen, Elizabeth. *The Heat of the Day*. London: Jonathan Cape, 1949.

Carrier, John W. 'A Jewish Proletariat', in *Explorations: An Annual on Jewish Themes*, ed. M. Mindlin and C. Bermant. Chicago: Quadrangle Books, 1968: 120–140.

Christie, Agatha. *Witness for the Prosecution and Other Stories*. London, New York: Dodd Mead, 1948.

Conrad, Joseph. *Victory*. New York: Doubleday and Co., 1915.

Dinesen, Isak (Karen Blixen-Finecke), "The Dreaming Child," in *Winter's Tales*. New York: Random House, 1942.

Dudley-Smith, Trevor [Elleston Trevor]. *The Berlin Memorandum*. London: Collins, 1965.

Fitzgerald, F. Scott. *The Last Tycoon*. New York: Charles Scribner's, 1941.

Fowles, John. *The French Lieutenant's Woman*. London: Jonathan Cape, 1969.

Green, F.L. *Odd Man Out*. London: Michael Joseph, 1945.

Hall, Adam. *The Berlin Memorandum*, London: Collins, 1965.

Hall, Peter. *Diaries*, ed. John Goodwin. London: Hamish Hamilton, 1983.

Hartley, L.P. *The Go-Between* London: Hamish Hamilton, 1953; Harmondsworth, Middlesex: Penguin Books, 1965.

Harwood, Ronald. *Taking Sides*. London: Faber & Faber, 1995.

Higgins, Aidan. *Helsingør Station & Other Departures: Fictions & Auto-biographies, 1956–1989*. London: Secker and Warburg, 1989.

—. *Langrishe Go Down*. London: John Calder, 1966.

Hoban, Russell. *Turtle Diary*. London: Cape, 1975.

Ishiguro, Kazuo. *The Remains of the Day*. London: Faber & Faber,1989.

James, Henry. *The Turn of the Screw*. London: Heineman, 1898.

Joyce, James. *Exiles*. London: Grant Richards Ltd., 1918.

—. *Finnegan's Wake*. London: Faber & Faber, 1939.

—. *Portrait of an Artist as a Young Man*. London: The Egoist Ltd., 1917.

—. *Ulysses*. Paris: Shakespeare and Co., 1921.

Kafka, Franz. *The Trial*. [London: Secker and Warburg (1937?)].

Kops, Bernard. *The World is a Wedding*. London: MacGibbon & Kee, 1963.

—. 'Whatever Happened to Isaac Babel' [Poem] in *Bernard Kops' East End: By the Waters of Whitechapel*. Nottingham: Five Leaves Publications, 2006.

Lipman, V. D. *Social History of the Jews in England 1850–1950*. London: Watts, 1954.

McEwen, Ian. *The Comfort of Strangers*. New York: Simon and Schuster, 1981.

Mamet, David. *Oleanna*. New York: Pantheon Books, 1992.

Maugham, Robin. *The Servant*. London: Falcon Press, 1948, republished London: Heineman, 1964.

Millar, Ronald. *Waiting for Gillian: A Play in Three Acts* from the novel *A Way through the Woods* by Nigel Balchin. London: S. French, 1954.

Mortimer, Penelope. [interview] *The Daily Telegraph* (3 September 1971): 11.

—. *The Pumpkin Eater*. London: Hutchinson, 1962.

Mosley, Nicholas, *Accident*, London: Hodder & Stoughton, 1965.

Nabokov, Vladimir. *Lolita*. Paris: Olympia Press, 1955.

Proust, Marcel. *À la Recherché du Temps Perdu* [1913]. Translated by C. K. Scott Moncrieff and Andreas Mayor. 12 vols. London: Chatto & Windus, [1922–1931].

Rattigan, Terence. *Separate Tables*. London: Hamilton, 1955.

Rose, Reginald. *Twelve Angry Men*. Chicago: Dramatic Pub. Co., 1955.

Sacks, Oliver. *Awakenings*. New York: Harper Perennial, 1973, 1990.

Salvador Dali and Luis Buñuel's 1924 silent film, *Un Chien Andalou*.

Sereny, Gitta, *Biography of Albert Speer*. New York: Knopf, 1995.

Shakespeare, William. *The Tragedy of King Lear* [c. 1605].

Shaw, Robert. *The Man in the Glass Booth*. New York: Harcourt, Brace & World, 1967.

Shaffer, Anthony. *Sleuth*. London: Calder & Boyars, 1971.

Shellard, Dominic, Steve Nicholson and Miriam Handley. *The Lord Chamberlain Regrets . . . A History of British Theatre Censorship*. London: The British Library, 2004.

Sherriff, R.C., *Journey's End*. New York: Brentano's, 1930.

Uhlman, Fred. *Reunion*. New York : Farrar, Straus and Giroux, 1977.

Vosper, Frank and Agatha Christie, *Love From a Stranger* (based on 'Philomel Cottage'). London: William Collins, 1936.

Wesker, Arnold. ' Chicken Soup With Barley', in *The Wesker Trilogy*. Harmondsworth, Middlesex: Penguin Books, 1960.

Index

Abraham 121
Abu Ghraib, Baghdad 131
Academy of Motion Pictures, Oscar 77
Aldgate 6
Aldgate East 25
Aldwych Theatre 59, 61, 78
Alexandra Theatre, Birmingham 35
Almeida Theatre 15, 112, 114, 116, 120, 124
America 15, 62, 98, 101, 126
American Embassy 95
Anderson, Michael 58
Ando, Roberto 3–4, 10, 14, 23
anti-Semitism 3, 18
Apollo Victoria Theatre, London 94
Aragay, Mireia 124
Archduke Ferdinand 127
Archibald, William: *The Innocents* 32
Areté 138
Argentina 71
Arts Theatre, London 35, 47
Ashcroft, Peggy 72, 92
Associated Rediffusion Television 59
Astbury, Anthony 87
Aston Villa 43–4
Astoria Dance Hall, Charing Cross Road 34
Atwood, Margaret: *The Handmaid's Tale* 101
Auden, W.H. 126

Bacall, Lauren 97
Bach, Johann Sebastian 38
Badcock, Jack (cricketer) 14
Baker, William 12, 18
Bakewell, Joan 37, 88–9

Bakewell, Michael 89
Bananas 134
Baptiste, Thomas 41
Barbados 92, 120–1
Barker, George 87
Baron, Alexander: *With Hope, Farewell* 17–18
Baron, David (Pinter as) 34
Basingstoke 48
Bates, Alan 76
Bates, Don (cricketer) 12
Battersea Public Reserve Library 32–3
Batty, Mark 12, 66
Beckett, Samuel 16
    Krapp's Last Tape 131
    Murphy 33
    Waiting for Godot 35
    Watt 32
Beethoven, Ludwig van 2, 10
    Fidelio 99
Beijing 81
Belfast 21
Bell, Mary Hayley: *The Uninvited Guest* 35
Bensky, Lawrence M. 17, 38, 49, 56
Ben-Zvi, Linda 86
Berenson, Bernard 112
Berlin 67
Berlin Memorandum, The (Hall) 67
Berry, Cicely 29
Besant, Walter: *The Eulogies of Richard Jefferies* 83
Bethnal Green 6
Bible 126
Billington, Michael 4, 16, 23–4, 29–33, 37–41, 43, 57, 61, 63,

67, 69, 71–2, 83–5, 89, 94,
103, 106, 108, 115–16, 120–1,
123–5, 131, 139n1, 155
Blair, Tony 70, 132
Blakely, Colin 79
Blanche, Bill 94
Blitz, the 10
Blixen, Karen (Dinesen, Isak) 107–8
The Dreaming Child 107–8
Winter's Tales 107
Boer War 78
BOMB 133–4
Boulogne 92
Boulton, James T. 57
Bournemouth Registry Office 36
Bournemouth Rep Company 35, 36
Bow 6
Bowen, Elizabeth 102
The Heat of the Day 102
Bowles, Peter 111–12
Brand, Daniel (HP's son) 43, 52, 53,
57, 60, 86, 87, 88, 116
Bray, Barbara 83
Brearley, Joseph 16, 20, 22, 23, 30, 61
Brecht, Bertolt: *The Mother* 34
Briggs, Johnny (cricketer) 13, 84
Brighton 116
Bristol 40, 42
Bristol University 43: Drama
Department 15, 39
British Broadcasting Corporation
(BBC) 29, 36, 40, 51, 70, 72,
82, 83–4, 85, 88, 92, 95, 132
British Film Academy Award 77
Best Screenplay 77
British Library (BL) 1, 21, 76, 113
British Politics 103
British Screenwriters Guild Award 58
Broadway 32, 57, 61, 70
Bryden, Ronald 79–80
Buñuel, Luis 21, 31
Un Chien Andalou 21
Burkman, Katherine H. 57, 71
*The Dramatic World of Harold
Pinter* 57
Bury, John 88

Caine, Michael 110
Cambridge 15, 38, 47
Cambridge, St. Catherine's College 15
Cambridge University 15, 23
Campden Hill 19
Cannes, Grande Prix Spécial du
Jury 69
Cannes Film Festival Palmes d'Or 77
Cardiff 61
Carné, Marcel: *Les Enfants du
Paradis* 20
Carrier, John W. 8
Catholic Aristocracy 87
Celine, Louis-Ferdinand 16, 20, 85
Central School of Speech and
Drama 29
Charing Cross Road 10–11, 34
Chesterfield 28
Chichester Festival Theatre 46
Chile 95
China 81: Cultural Revolution 81
Chiswick 19, 54
Chiswick High Road 43, 57:373
Chiswick High Road 52–3
Christie Agatha: *Love from a
Stranger* 35; *Witness for the
Prosecution* 35
Christie, Julie 76
Ciment, Michel 100
Clapton Pond 5, 8, 20
Coalmont, Illinois 106
Coate Farmhouse 83
Codron, Michael 43, 52
Colchester Rep 35
Comedy Theatre 75, 112
Commercial Road 6
Communists 3, 17, 61, 85
Compton, Denis (cricketer) 12
Concentration Camps 71
Connaught Theatre, Worthing 35
Conrad, Joseph 97, 126
Victory 97
Cooper, Gary 126
Copenhagen 108
Cornwall, evacuation to 9, 127
honeymoon 36–7

Cote d'Azur 79
Cottesloe Theatre 91–2, 93, 112, 127
Covent Garden Press 86
Crabbe, Kerry Lee 132
cricket 10, 11–14, 18, 35, 61, 78
Crystal Palace 92
Cuckfield 92
Cusack, Cyril 22

Daily Express 87
Daily Mail 61
Daily Telegraph, The 46, 60
Daily Telegraph Magazine 11, 12
Daish, Judy 43
Dali, Salvador 21
Dalston 8, 17, 57
Danish 107
Darges, Manohla 110
de Jongh, Nicholas 128
Dench, Judi 93, 94
Dickson, Wheeler Winston 69
Dignam, Mark 92
Dillinger, John 126
Dinesen, Isak *see* Blixen, Karen
Donner, Clive 57
Dorset 91, 121, 124–5
Dos Passos, John Roderigo 16, 85, 126
Dublin 19, 130
Dublin Gate Theatre Pinter
        Festival 32, 117
Duchess Theatre 52
Dudley-Smith, Trevor *see* Trevor,
        Elleston
du Garde Peach, L. 34

Eastbourne 14, 34–5
East End, London 6, 7, 18, 61, 79, 91
Edrich, Bill (cricketer) 12
Eichmann, Adolf 70–1
Eliot, Thomas Stearns 31, 38, 126
        The Waste Land 31
Embassy Theatre, Swiss Cottage 34
Encounter 38
Engel, Susan 42
England 2–3, 12, 13, 17, 58, 63, 103,
        108, 121

Epsom 61–2
Esau 121
Essex Road 57
Esslin, Martin 26, 40, 43, 51, 120, 127
        *The Peopled Wound: The Work of
                Harold Pinter* 139n3
        Pinter: A Study of His Plays 40,
                43, 51
        The Pinter Review 105, 116, 120
Europa Theatre Prize 130
Evening Standard 47, 52, 128
        Drama Award 52
Everett, Rupert 102
Eyre Methuen 86

Faber & Faber 131, 134
Fairmead Court, Kew 57
Fascist/ism 5, 6, 17, 22, 61, 85
Faulkner, William 126
Feinstein, Elaine 38
Feld, De la 22
Fen District 116
Film Comment 100
Financial Times 123
Finsbury Park 20
First World War 15, 21, 78, 84, 98, 101
Fitzgerald, F. Scott: *The Last Tycoon* 84
Flanagan, Pauline 31
Fleet Street 38
Florence 112
Florence, Peter 21, 58, 60
Flourish 38
Ford, Anna 95
Foster, Barry 29, 31
Foster, Frank (cricketer) 13, 84
Fowles, John 21, 90
        The French Lieutenant's Woman
                (1981) 21, 90
Fox, Edward 76, 111–12
France 20, 128
Franklin, Rose *see* Moskowitz, Rose
Fraser, Lady Antonia (HP's second
        wife) 67, 86–8, 95, 116, 118,
        121, 124, 130–1, 134–6
French Legion d'Honneur 130
Furtwängler, Wilhelm 111

Gable, Clark 126
Gaelic 121
Gaieties Cricket Club 13
Gale, Steven 58, 69, 90, 105, 106,
       139n3
Gambon, Michael 17, 88, 102
Gardiner, C. Wrey 29
Genesis 121
German/s 7, 10, 71, 82, 99, 101, 102,
       138
Germany 8, 9, 14, 68, 99–100, 111,
       121
Gershwin, George 59, 80
Gestapo 105
Giacometti, Alberto 16, 85
Gielgud, Sir John 84, 85
Gillen, Francis 105, 108, 116, 120,
       139n4
Goethe, Johann Wolfgang von 101
Golders Green 8
Goldstein, Michael (Mick) 16, 35
Graham, William Sydney 26, 87
Granada Television 102
Granta 26
Gray, Simon: *Butley* 88
       The Late Middle Class 111
       Life Support 111
       Old Masters 111–12
Green, F.L. *Old Man Out* 21
Greville Press 87, 134
Grey, Anthony 81
Grimes, Charles 115
Guardian 16, 22, 134, 136, 137
Guatemala 95
Guild of British Television Producers,
       Directors 59
Gulf Wars 113, 133
Gussow, Mel 90

Hackney 1, 2, 5, 6, 7, 8, 19, 21, 24,
       28, 32, 35, 37, 48, 54, 66,
       126, 132
Hackney Boys' Club 16
Hackney Downs 10–11, 15, 20, 23
Hackney Downs Grammar School
       10–11, 15, 23

Hackney Downs School Magazine 11,
       18, 20, 22, 134
Hackney Library 25
Hall, Adam 67, 80
Hall, David 52
Hall, Sir Peter 12, 35, 59, 61,
       66, 71, 72, 74, 78, 79, 84,
       88, 92
Hamlett, Dilys 30
Hampshire County Cricket Club 12
Hampstead Theatre 46
Hanover Terrace, Regent's Park 67
Hardstaff, Joseph (cricketer) 11
Hardy, Thomas 126
'Harold Pinta' 28, 29, 134
Hart, Lorenz 80
Hartley, L.P.: *The Go-Between* 12, 21,
       76–8
Harwood, Ronald: *Taking Sides* 111
Havel, Vaclav 105
Hayman, Ronald 12, 75, 76
Hebrew 121
Hemingway, Ernest 126
Hendon 55
Heriot, Charles D. 72
Hickey, William 87
Higgins, Aidan: *Helsing for
       Station* 82
       Langrishe Go Down 36, 82
Hiroshima 16
Hirst, George (cricketer) 13, 84, 116
Hitler, Adolph 8, 10, 15, 25, 100,
       101, 121
Hitler Youth Movement 100
Hoban, Russel: *Turtle Diary* 97–8
Hobson, Harold 25, 43, 47, 74
Hodge, Patricia 88, 102
Holiday, Billie 80
Hollywood 58, 84, 126
Holm, Ian 116
Holocaust 16, 71, 101
Hopkins, Anthony 104
Hove Town Hall 5, 135
Huddersfield Rep 35
Hudgins, Christopher C. 106, 107
Hutton, Sir Leonard (cricketer) 12

Ilkley Literature Festival 26
Independent 134
Independent on Sunday 109
Inter-marriage 63
International Court of Justice 95
Intimate Theatre, Palmer's Green,
        North London 35
Iraq 123, 130, 132
Ireland 19, 24, 31–3, 34, 82
Irish 12, 19, 31, 32, 48, 121, 126
Irishman 42
Irons, Jeremy 17, 82, 88
Isaac 121
Ishiguro, Kuzuo: *The Remains of the
        Day* 107
Isis (river) 69
Islington 7, 15
Israel 71, 103

Jackson, Glenda 98
Jacob 121
James, Henry: 'The Turn of the Screw' 32
Jefferies, Richard 83
Jerusalem 57, 70
Jewish 3, 5–8, 10, 16, 17, 18, 41, 48,
        49, 105, 126
    Bar Mitzvah 4
    Passover 4
    synagogue 4
    Yom Kippur 36–7
Jewish Chronicle 15, 54, 62
Jhabvala, Ruth Prawer 107
Johnson, Jill 35
Jones, David 82, 88, 104, 105
Joseph, Stephen 29
Joyce, James 128
    Exiles 78
    Finnegan's Wake 19
    A Portrait of the Artist 18
    Ulysses 11, 18–19
June 20th Society 95

Kafka, Franz 130
    The Trial 104–5
Karl Alexander Gymnasium,
        Stuttgart 99

Kazan, Elia 84
Kern, Jerome 80
Kew 57
Kilburn 88, 132
Kingsley, Ben 88, 98
King's Theatre Hammersmith 33, 36
Kitchen, Michael 92
Kolin, Bohemia 105
Kops, Bernard
    Bernard Kops' East End 7, 25
    'Whatever Happened to Isaac
        Babel?' 7
    The World is a Wedding 6
Kray Brothers 61
Kubrick, Stanley 106
Kurds 95

Lamarr, Hedy 126
Larkin, Philip 87
Laurel and Hardy 113
Law, Jude 110
Lawrence, D.H. 126
Lea River 8
Lehmann, Beatrix 47
Leigh, Vivien 36
Leighton, Margaret 76, 77
Lester, Richard 97
Leveaux, David 120
Limehouse 6
Lipman, V.D. 6
Lipstein, Isidor (HP's uncle) 3
Lipstein, Sophie (née Pinter; HP's
        aunt) 3, 4
Lipstein, Sue (HP's cousin) 3
Little John [pub], Chiswick 53
London 2, 3, 4, 5, 7, 8, 9, 10, 16, 18,
        19, 20, 26, 31, 33, 34, 38, 46,
        47, 55, 61, 69, 80, 81, 91, 102,
        121, 127, 138
London Docklands 7
London Review of Books 134
Lord Chamberlain's Office 72
Lords Cricket Ground 11
Losey, Joseph 68, 69, 77, 83
    'The Servant: Notes on the Film' 58
Luton 55

Lyall, Sarah: 'Art and Leisure' 87, 110
Lyceum Theatre, Broadway 57
Lyme Regis, Dorset 91
Lynch, Finbar 46
Lyne, Adrian 106
Lyon, Sue 106
Lyric Theatre, Hammersmith 47, 51, 94
Lyttleton Theatre, National
    Theatre 16, 128

Macaulay, Alastair 123
McEwen, Ian: *The Comfort of
    Strangers* 101, 102–3
McLaughlin, Kyle 104
McMaster, Anew 31, 33
McGilvray, Alan 12
McWhinnie, Donald 51, 52
Mamet, David 106
Manchester 36
Manchester Guardian 52
Mann, Joe *see* Moskowitz, Judah
Mann, Richard *see* Moskowitz, Harry
Manor House 20
Marble Arch 38
Marcus, David 32
Marks, Louis 104–5
Marx Brothers 31
Mason, James 21, 81, 106
Massey, Anna 93
Massey, Daniel 88
Maudsley Hospital 46
Maugham, Robin: *The Servant* 36, 38,
    57, 58–9, 69–70
Mecca 57
Merchant, Vivien 36–7, 59, 60, 75,
    79, 86, 92, 134
Merchant-Ivory Productions 107
Mermaid Theatre, London 78
Miller, Arthur 94–5
Miller, Henry 16
Mirren, Helen 88, 103
Mixed Doubles 75
Modern Drama 57
Monty Python 46
Moore, Stephen 46

Mortimer, Penelope: *The Pumpkin
    Eater* 60
Moskowitz, Fay (HP's aunt) 3
Moskowitz, Harry (HP's maternal
    grandfather) 3
Moskowitz, Judah (HP's uncle) 4
Moskowitz, Lou (HP's uncle) 4
Moskowitz, Rose (née Franklin; HP's
    maternal grandmother) 3
Mosley, Nicholas: *Accident* 68–70
Mosley, Sir Osward 5–6, 8, 18
Mussolini, Benito 127

Nabokov, Vladimir: *Lolita* 106–7
Nagasaki 16
National Liberal Club, London 34
National Student Drama Festival 40
National Theatre, London 12, 15, 16,
    46, 84, 88, 92, 93, 95
Nazi 5, 16, 20, 98, 99–100, 101, 102,
    111, 121, 124
Nelson, Mr. (teacher) 9
Neruda, Pablo 132
New Arts Theatre, London 35–6
Newton, Robert 22, 80
New York 70, 98
New Yorker 8, 9, 10
New York Film Critics' Best Writing
    Award 58
New York Lincoln Center Pinter
    Festival 112
New York Review of Books 134
New York Times 87, 110, 123
New York West Village 133–4
Nicaragua 95, 132
Norfolk 78
North Circular Road 55
North London 6–7, 11, 15, 35, 55, 61
Northwest London 8
Norwich 78
Notting Hill Gate 43
Nuclear War 94

Observer, The 24, 52, 79, 134
Odessa, Ukraine 3

Ohio State University, Columbus,
 Ohio 115
Old Testament, The 105
Old Vic 84, 111
Old Vic Drama School 30
Olivier, Sir Laurence 109
Ormond, Julia 107–8
Oxford 47, 68, 69, 70, 88
Oxford Street, London 34
Oxford University 23
 Magdalen College 69, 116

Palace Court Theatre,
 Bournemouth 35
Paris 3, 86
Paris Review 17, 38, 49
Parks, the, Oxford 69
Passos, John Dos 16, 85, 126
Peacock, Keith 101
Pearson, Richard 47
PEN 11, 95, 111
Percival, Ron 16, 22
Peter, John 128
Pinta, Harold 28, 29, 134
Pinter, Daniel *see* Brand, Daniel
Pinter, Dolly (HP's aunt) 3
Pinter, Fanny (née Baron; HP's paternal
 grandmother) 2, 4
Pinter, Frances (née Moskowitz;
 HP's mother) 2, 3, 10, 31, 36,
 98, 116
Pinter, Harold
 and Antonia Fraser 67, 86–8, 116,
  133, 136
  betrayal 14–17, 21, 37, 53,
   88–90
 as conscientious objector 25–6
 contribution to school magazine 18–20; cricket 10, 11–14
 as 'David Baron' 34
 and Dilys Hamlett 30
 divorce from Vivien 87
 and Donald Wolfit 33, 111, 134
 drama schools 29, 30
 early childhood 11, 84
 family 1–5, 36–7, 92

first marriage 36–7
friendship 11, 14–17, 37, 100–1
and W.S. Graham 26
as 'Harold Pinta' 28, 29, 134
Ireland 31–3, 34, 82
and James Joyce 10–11, 18, 19,
 78
and Joan Bakewell 37, 88–9
Judaism 4
memory 6, 11, 17, 30, 31, 37,
 66, 77–81, 83, 84, 89, 107, 109
Nobel Prize 130
only criminal act 33
opposition to bullies 22
Pauline Flanagan 31
poetry 19–20, 28, 32, 49–50, 93,
 127
politics 94–5, 96–7, 103, 104
relationships to parents 5, 29,
 103
as reviser 53, 54, 109, 110
and Samuel Beckett 32, 33,
 35, 131
and Shakespeare 26–7, 109
and son Daniel 43, 53, 60, 86, 87
time 76, 77, 78–1, 84, 89, 99,
 128, 131
Vivien Merchant 36–7, 92
as actor 22, 29, 31, 46, 82, 98,
 109–111, 116, 128, 130–131
as director
 Ashes to Ashes 71, 112, 120–4,
  127, 135, 137
 Butley (Gray) 88
 Celebration 15, 34, 112, 124–7,
  134
 Exiles (Joyce) 78
 The Hothouse 15, 46
 The Late Middle Classes
  (Gray) 111
 Life Support (Gray) 111
 The Man in the Glass Booth
  (Shaw) 70–1
 Mountain Language 46, 95–6,
  112, 124, 131, 137
 The New World Order 112, 113

Pinter, Harold (*Cont'd*)
  The Old Masters (Gray) 111–12
  Oleanna (Mamet) 110–11
  Party Time 112, 114–16
  Sweet Bird of Youth
    (Williams) 96–7
  Taking Sides (Harwood) 111
  Twelve Angry Men (Rose) 111
  collections of work
    Collected Poems and Prose 20, 134
    Collected Screenplays 60
    Five Screenplays 78
    Plays Four 86
    Poems (1968, 1971) 27, 35
    Six Poems for A 87, 136, 138
    Various Voices 12, 14, 26–32, 38,
      40, 48, 50, 87, 103, 124, 133,
      139
    War 132–3, 134, 135, 136
  interviews (conversations)
    Anna Ford 95
    Christopher Hudgins 106, 107
    Francis Gillen 105
    Kenneth Cavander 58
    Kenneth Tynan 40
    Kirsty Wark 137
    Lawrence Bensky 17, 38, 49, 56
    Louis Marks 104–5
    Mel Gussow 90
    Michele Ciment 100
    Mireia Arágay 124
    Peter Florence 21, 58, 60
    with Roberto Ando 3, 4, 10,
      14, 23
    Royal Court Theatre (2005) 33
    Sarah Lyall 87, 110
    Steve Gale 58, 69, 90, 105, 106,
      139n3
  plays
    Ashes to Ashes 71, 108, 112, 120–4,
      127, 135, 137
    The Basement 70
    Betrayal 14–15, 21, 37, 88–90
    The Birthday Party 3, 6, 7, 14, 25,
      35, 43, 46, 47–51, 56, 63, 86,
      96, 113

The Caretaker (*The Guest*) 4, 5, 42,
  49, 52–7, 58, 61, 76, 96
Celebration 15, 34, 112, 124–7
The Collection 58, 59
The Dumb Waiter 7, 14, 39,
  43–4, 46
The Dwarfs 5, 16, 37–8, 43, 132,
  138
Family Voices 35, 59, 92
The Homecoming 1, 3, 5, 15, 22, 34,
  37, 49, 59, 60–6, 67, 71, 79,
  94, 116–17, 123, 128
The Hothouse 15, 16, 46, 111
A Kind of Alaska 59, 92, 93–4
Landscape 36, 43, 44, 70, 71–4, 79,
  117, 124, 127
The Lover 35, 57, 59–60
Mixed Doubles 75
monologue 15, 16, 36, 42, 85–6
Moonlight 112, 116–20, 127
Mountain Language 46, 95–6, 112,
  114, 124, 131, 137
Night 74, 75–6
A Night Out 51, 63
Night School 36
No Man's Land 13, 17, 43, 84–5,
  116, 128
Old Times 21, 30, 59, 75, 78–81,
  114, 124, 127, 128
One for the Road 94–5, 124
Other Places (triple bill) 92
Party Time 112, 114–16
Precisely 94–5
The Room 7, 14, 15, 33, 39–43, 45,
  46, 112, 124, 125, 127
Silence 12, 36, 44, 74–5, 79
A Slight Ache 14, 39, 44–6, 127
Something in Common (un-produced
  radio play) 44
Victoria Station 3, 59, 92–3
The Play's the Thing 7, 131
poems:
  collections:
    Collected Poems and Prose 20, 134
    100 Poems by 100 Poets 87
    I Know the Place 87, 93

99 Poems in Translation 87
Poems (1968, 1971) 35
Poems by Harold Pinter 133, 136
Poems by Philip Larkin 87
Six Poems for A 87, 136, 138
Ten Early Poems 134
individual poems
  'Afternoon' 137
  'American Football' 133, 136
  'Body' 137
  'The Bombs' 136
  'Cancer Cells' 133, 136
  'Chandeliers and Shadows' 28, 29
  'Dawn' 134
  'Death (Births and Deaths
    Registration Act, 1953)' 4–5,
    103, 132, 133, 135
  'Democracy' 132–3, 136
  'Episode' 32
  'The Error of Alarm' 137
  'Ghost' 134–5
  'God Bless America' 136
  'Gulf War' 133
  'I Know the Place' 87, 93
  'I Shall Tear Off My Terrible
    Cap' 28, 29
  'The Islands of Aran Seen from
    the Moher Cliffs' 32, 127
  'Joseph Brearley (1909–1977)' 20
  'Later (1974)' 137
  'New Year in the Midlands' 28,
    29
  'O Beloved Maiden' 19
  'One a Story, Two a Death' 28
  'Paris' 134
  'Poem (1953)' 32
  'Poem (1986)' 12
  'Poem (2007)' 87
  'Requiem for 1945' 133
  'School Life' 19, 23
  'The Special Relationship' 136
  'To My Wife' 136
  'A View of the Party' 50
  'Weather Forecast' 136
screenplays
  Accident 68–70

Betrayal 102
The Caretaker 4, 5, 42, 49, 52–7,
  58, 61, 76, 96
The Comfort of Strangers 101, 102–3
The Dreaming Child 107–8
The French Lieutenant's Woman 21,
  90–1
The Go-Between 12, 21, 76–8, 83
The Handmaid's Tale 101
The Heat of the Day 102
King Lear 109
Langrishe Go Down 36, 82–3
The Last Tycoon 84
Lolita 106–7
The Proust Screenplay (*Remembrance
  of Things Past*) 83–4, 89
The Pumpkin Eater 60
The Quiller Memorandum 67–8
The Remains of the Day 107
Reunion 14, 21, 68, 71, 82,
  98–101, 103
The Servant 36, 38, 57, 58–9, 69
Sleuth 78, 109–11
The Trial 104–5
Turtle Diary 97–8
Victory 97
speeches/talks
  Art Truth & Politics 131
  'Realism and Post Realism in the
    French Cinema' 20
  Turin Speech 132
  'Writing for the Theatre' 40
writings (novel, short stories,
  sketches, letters)
  Apart from That 130–1
  'Arthur Wellard' 13
  'The Black and White' 38
  'Blood Sports' 19
  The Catch a Correspondence 13
  The Dwarfs (novel) 5, 16, 37–8,
    43, 132, 138
  The Examination 38
  'First Draft *The Homecoming*' 1,
    3, 5, 15, 22, 34, 37, 49, 59,
    60–6, 67, 71, 79, 94, 116–17,
    123, 128, 139n4

'James Joyce' 18, 78
Jimmy 17
Kullus (prose poem) 27
(letters): to William Baker 12, 18
Mac 31
'Memories of Cricket' 11
'The Mirror' 137–8
Nobel Lecture 131–33
'A Note on Shakespeare' 26–7
The Play's the Thing 7, 131
Press Conference 112, 128
'The Queen of all the Fairies' 24,
    30
'Sketches' 112
'Tess' 112, 128–9
Sunday Times 25, 43, 47, 56, 74,
    128, 133
Pinter, Jack (HP's father) 2–5, 8–9,
    25, 29, 132, 135
Pinter, Mary (HP's aunt) 3
Pinter, Nathan (HP's paternal
    grandfather) 2
Pinter, Rachel (HP's aunt) 2
Pinter, Sophie *see* Lipstein, Sophie
Pinter Archive (British Library) 76, 113
Pinter Review, The 105, 120
Pleasance, Donald 54
Poetry Ireland 32
Poetry London 28, 29, 134
Poetry Quarterly 28, 29
Poland 2, 3
Port Stewart, Co. Londonderry 35
Pound, Ezra 126
Prague 105, 130
Prix Italia 59
Promenade Concerts 81
Prospect 38
Proust, Marcel 83, 84, 89, 127–8
    À la Recherché du Temps Perdu 21, 82
Purcell Room 87

Racism 55, 97
Raine, Craig 1, 138
Rattigan, Terence: *Separate Tables* 37, 39
Redgrave, Sir Michael 76

Reed, Carol 81
    Odd Man Out 21
Regent's Park 19, 67, 78
Reisz, Karel 90, 101
Reuters 81
Richardson, Natasha 102
Richardson, Sir Ralph 84
Ridley Road 17, 18
Robards, Jason 98, 99, 101, 104
Robin Hood [pub], Chiswick 53
Rogers, Paul 93
Rogers, Richard 80
Rose, Reginald: *Twelve Angry
    Men* 111
Rosselli, John 52
Roth, Tim 109
Royal Academy of Dramatic Art
    (RADA) 23, 24–5, 29
Royal Court Theatre 7, 33, 111, 112,
    123: Upstairs 112, 131
Royal National Theatre 92
Royal Shakespeare Company 59, 70,
    72, 74, 78
Rumsey, Fred (cricketer) 12, 75
Russian 81

Sacks, Oliver: *Awakenings* 93, 94
Saskatchewan, University of 15
Saturday Guardian 137
St. Ives 26
St. John's Wood High Street 138
St. Martin's Theatre, London 70
St. Paul's School 116
Salmon Lane 6
Scarborough 29
Schatzberg, Jerry 14, 98
Schiller, J.C. Friedrich von 101
Schnabel, Artur 2, 4
Schrader, Paul L. 102
Second World War 4, 22, 61, 92, 99,
    124, 131
Sellers, Peter 106
Sereny, Gitta 121
Shaffer, Anthony 110
    Sleuth 78, 109

Shakespeare, William 22, 26–7, 30–1,
    109
    Hamlet 31
    Henry VIII 29
    King Lear 31, 109, 116
    Macbeth 22, 71
    Othello 31, 82
    Romeo and Juliet 22
    Twelfth Night 30
Shaw, Robert 70–1
Shellard, Dominic 72
Shepherd's Bush Green 138
Sherriff, R.C.: *Journey's End* 21
Shoreditch 6, 8
Shulman, Milton 47
Sidcup 57
Simó, Ramon 124
Simpson, Reg (cricketer) 11
Slater, John 47
Smith, Auriol 39
Smith, Ian 95
    Pinter in the Theatre 25
Smith, R.D. 23, 29, 34
Soho Square 20
Somerset County Cricket Club 13
South Bank 86, 87, 92, 112
Soviet Union 25
Spectator 132
Speer, Albert 121
Spencer, Charles 46
Spiegel, Sam 84, 88
Spooner, R.H. (cricketer) 13, 84, 85
Stage, The 31
Stalin, Joseph 3
Stamford Hill 8
Stepney 2, 6, 8
Stock, Nigel 75
Stoke Newington 2, 5, 7
Stoke-on-Trent 29
Stokesley 13
Stratford-upon-Avon 19
Streep, Meryl 91
Stuttgart 98, 99, 100, 101
Sunday Times 25, 43, 47, 56, 74,
    128, 133

Supple, Barry 15, 23, 54, 62, 63, 64
Sussex Coast 5, 57
    County Cricket Club 12

Tambimuttu, J.M. 28
Tatler 112, 128
Taxi-drivers 15, 101
Taylor, John Russell 7
Thames 8
Theatre Royal, Haymarket 97
Theatre Royal, Waterford 82
Theatres Act (1968) 72
Thistlewaite Road 2, 8, 34, 41
Thomas, Dylan 23, 29, 126
Thomson, Ada *see* Merchant, Vivien
Times Literary Supplement 103, 123,
    134, 135
Torquay 39: Torquay rep. 37
Tottenham (North London) 3
Transatlantic Review 38, 58
Treves, Di 127
Trevor, Elleston 67
Tricycle Theatre, Kilburn 132
Turin 1, 130, 132
Turkey 94, 95
Tutin, Dorothy 79, 114
Tynan, Kenneth 40, 52
Tzara, Tristan 16

Uhlman, Fred: *Reunion* 14, 21, 68, 82,
    98–101
United States 57, 101
    foreign policy 131
    London Embassy 132
    United States Ambassador
        (Turkey) 95
    United States in Nicaragua 95
University of Barcelona 124

Vaesen, Guy 35–6, 53
Vanunu, Mordecai 103
Venice 90, 102, 103
Victorian England 108
Victoria Park 6
Victoria Station 3, 59, 92–3

'Viva Pinter', Lyons 1, 88
Walken, Christopher 102–3
Wark, Kirsty 137
Warwick 87
Waterford 82
Watford 55
Wax, Emmanuel 17, 42–3, 84
Webster, John 17, 85
    The Duchess of Malfi 29–30
    The White Devil 16
Wellard, Arthur 13
Wembley 121
Wernick, Morris 24, 25, 62, 63, 132
Wesker, Arnold: *Chicken Soup with
    Barley* 6
West Brompton, London 33
West End 52
West End Stage 59
West London 88
Whitbread Ale 28
Whitby 34
White, Harry 32
Whitechapel 6
    Road 7
    Whitechapel Library, Aldgate East 25

Wilfred Owen Award Party 130
Wilkinson, Alan 13
Williams, Mrs. 9
Williams, Tennessee: *Sweet Bird of
    Youth* 97
Wilton, Penelope 17, 88, 129
Windermere, Lake 91
Winters, Shelley 106
Wolfit, Sir Donald 33, 109, 111
Wood, Peter 47, 48
Woolf, Henry 11, 15–17, 18, 22, 25,
    34, 39, 85, 86, 137
    'My Sixty Years in Harold's
    Gang' 16, 37
World War I 15, 21, 78, 84, 98, 101
Worthing 19, 31, 35, 60, 61: 14
    Ambrose Place 57

Yardley, Norman (cricketer) 12
Yeats, William Butler: 'Lapis Lazuli' 31
York, Michael 102
York, Susannah 94
Yugoslavia 123

Zionism 101, 103